Better Homes and Gardens®

LOW-CALORIE
MICROWAVE
COOK BOOK

© Copyright 1984 by Meredith Corporation, Des Moines, Iowa.
All Rights Reserved. Printed in the United States of America.
First Edition. Second Printing, 1985.
Library of Congress Catalog Card Number: 84-60799
ISBN: 0-696-01450-5

BETTER HOMES AND GARDENS® BOOKS

Editor: Gerald M. Knox
Art Director: Ernest Shelton
Managing Editor: David A. Kirchner

Food and Nutrition Editor: Nancy Byal
Department Head—Cook Books: Sharyl Heiken
Associate Department Heads: Sandra Granseth,
    Rosemary C. Hutchinson, Elizabeth Woolever
Senior Food Editors: Julie Henderson, Julia Malloy,
    Marcia Stanley
Associate Food Editors: Jill Burmeister,
    Molly Culbertson, Linda Foley, Linda Henry,
    Lynn Hoppe, Mary Jo Plutt, Maureen Powers,
    Joyce Trollope
Recipe Development Editor: Marion Viall
Test Kitchen Director: Sharon Stilwell
Test Kitchen Home Economists: Jean Brekke,
    Kay Cargill, Marilyn Cornelius, Maryellyn Krantz,
    Lynelle Munn, Dianna Nolin, Marge Steenson,
    Cynthia Volcko

Associate Art Directors: Linda Ford Vermie,
    Neoma Alt West, Randall Yontz
Copy and Production Editors: Marsha Jahns,
    Mary Helen Schiltz, Carl Voss, David A. Walsh
Assistant Art Directors: Harijs Priekulis, Tom Wegner
Senior Graphic Designers: Alisann Dixon,
    Lynda Haupert, Lyne Neymeyer
Graphic Designers: Mike Burns, Mike Eagleton,
    Deb Miner, Stan Sams, D. Greg Thompson,
    Darla Whipple, Paul Zimmerman

Vice President, Editorial Director: Doris Eby
Executive Director, Editorial Services: Duane L. Gregg

General Manager: Fred Stines
Director of Publishing: Robert B. Nelson
Vice President, Retail Marketing: Jamie Martin
Vice President, Direct Marketing: Arthur Heydendael

Low-Calorie Microwave Cook Book

Editors: Lynn Hoppe, Marcia Stanley
Copy and Production Editor: Carl Voss
Graphic Designer: Paul Zimmerman
Electronic Text Processor: Joyce Wasson

On the front cover:

Hot Shrimp Salad (see recipe, page 70)

Our seal assures you that every recipe in *Low-Calorie Microwave Cook Book* has been tested by the Better Homes and Gardens® Test Kitchen. This means that each recipe is practical and reliable, and meets our high standards of taste appeal.

Microwave Cooking Minus Calories

Did you know that as a calorie counter, you have an advantage because you own a microwave oven? This idea may be new to you, but when you think about it, many of the built-in qualities of microwave cooking complement the goals of dieters.

For instance, you can use a microwave oven to cook many foods without additional fat. Because microwave cooking has less of a·drying effect on foods than conventional cooking, added fat, with its many calories, is often not needed.

Similarly, many foods, such as vegetables, require little or no additional water when cooked in the microwave oven. In addition to better nutrient retention, this results in enhanced appetite appeal.

Curried Pork
and Tomatoes
(see recipe, page 18)

Microwave Cooking Minus Calories

The improved color, taste, and texture make naturally low-calorie vegetables even more enjoyable.

And of course, convenience is just as important to dieters as it is to everybody else. After all, less time spent in the kitchen means less temptation to nibble!

As you can see, your microwave oven has a lot of calorie-cutting potential. In this book, we've put that potential to work to create delicious, low-calorie recipes to help you diet with aplomb.

Good Sense Reducing

Whether you grimace at your reflection in a full-length mirror or you just want to trim a few inches from your waist, you already have taken the first step in reducing. You have recognized a need to lose weight.

You probably already know from personal experience that the relationship between food intake and body weight strikes a delicate balance. Take in more calories than you expend, and you will gain weight. Fortunately, the converse also is true.

Before starting a diet, consult with your physician to plan a program that will result in a weight loss of about 1 to 2 pounds per week. Studies show that slow, steady progress yields the best long-term results.

To lose any weight, you must consume fewer calories than you burn. That is, you must have a calorie deficit. To lose 1 pound of fat per week, you need a 3,500-calorie deficit. This equals a daily deficit of 500 calories.

As you take in fewer calories, remember to pay particular attention to your nutritional needs. Planning to make every calorie a worthwhile source of nutrients is especially important to the dieter.

The opposite of calorie intake is calorie expenditure. Exercise burns calories, improves fitness, and provides mental relaxation.

Try making reasonable lifestyle changes that include more physical activity in your daily routine. Something as simple as parking your car farther from your destination increases energy expenditure.

No matter how much weight you lose, the real challenge comes in keeping the weight off. If you go back to your former way of eating, you'll eventually go back to your former weight. The key to continued success is in permanently adopting some of the life-style changes you made while reducing.

Basic Five Food Groups

A sensible approach to dieting restricts your caloric intake, but does not deprive you of nutrients. Use the Basic Five Food Groups to help you select a variety of foods which will offer the greatest variety of nutrients.

Vegetable and Fruit Group

The vegetable and fruit group provides vitamins A and C, as well as other nutrients and fiber. A balanced diet should include four daily servings from this group. One-half cup of fruit or vegetable, one orange, or a medium potato count as one serving.

Bread and Cereal Group

Foods from the bread and cereal group are important sources of iron, thiamine, niacin, and riboflavin. Fortified breakfast cereals also are good sources of vitamins B_{12}, C, and D.

Include four servings from the bread and cereal group every day. A serving equals one slice of bread; ½ to ¾ cup cooked cereal, noodles, or rice; or 1 ounce ready-to-eat cereal. Select whole grain or enriched forms to improve the nutrient quality.

Milk and Cheese Group

Milk and cheese products are major sources of calcium. These products also provide riboflavin, protein, and vitamins A, B_6, B_{12}, and usually vitamin D.

One 8-ounce glass of milk, 1 cup plain yogurt, 1⅓ ounces hard cheese, or 2 cups cottage cheese equals one serving from the milk and cheese group. Daily recommendations from this group are two servings for adults; three servings for children through 12 years of age; and four servings for teens, pregnant women, and nursing mothers. For dieters, skim milk, low-fat yogurt, buttermilk, and low-fat cottage cheese are especially good choices.

Meat, Poultry, Fish, Nuts, and Beans Group

The foods in this group supply protein, iron, thiamine, niacin, riboflavin, and phosphorus.

Plan two servings daily, varying the sources. One serving equals 2 to 3 ounces of lean, cooked meat, poultry, or fish, all without bone; 2 eggs; or 1 cup cooked dried beans, peas, soybeans, or lentils. Or, 2 tablespoons peanut butter or ¼ to ½ cup nuts equal one-half serving.

For cutting calories, choose lean cuts of meats such as lean ground beef, beef round steaks or roasts, pork loin roasts or chops, and veal.

Fats, Sweets, and Alcohol Group

Foods in the fats, sweets, and alcohol group are high in calories and provide low levels of vitamins, minerals, or protein per calorie. Butter, mayonnaise, salad dressings, sugar, soft drinks, and alcoholic drinks are in this group. Try to minimize foods from this group.

Nutrition Analysis

For your convenience in planning menus, we have included, on pages 91-93, a nutrition analysis of all recipes in this book. The analysis includes the calorie count and the number of grams of protein, carbohydrate, and fat in one serving. The analysis also gives the percentages of United States Recommended Daily Allowances (U.S. RDA) for certain nutrients.

The primary source of information for the nutrition analyses comes from a computerized method using Agriculture Handbook No. 456 by the United States Department of Agriculture.

To obtain this information, we made some assumptions:
● We omitted garnishes and ingredients listed as optional in the ingredient list from our analyses.
● We based calculations for main-dish meat recipes on values for cooked, lean meat, trimmed of separable fat.
● When two ingredient options appear in a recipe, we calculated the nutrition analysis using the first choice of ingredients.
● When an ingredient has a variable weight (such as a 1- to 1½-pound beef sirloin steak), we based the analysis on the lesser weight.

7

Microwave Cooking Minus Calories

Using Your Microwave Oven

Now that we have reviewed the basics of good-sense reducing, let's review the basics of microwave cooking.

Variable Power

Variable power means that a microwave oven has more power settings than on and off. Microwave ovens with variable power achieve power settings lower than 100% (such as 10%, 30%, 50%, and 70%) by cycling microwave energy on and off during the cooking time. Most newer ovens have from two to ten settings.

The settings on microwave ovens and the percent of power assigned to these settings vary from brand to brand. Therefore, you must determine which setting on your oven corresponds to what percent of power.

For microwave ovens with numbered settings, just multiply the power setting by ten to get the percent of power. A power setting of five corresponds to 50% power.

For microwave ovens with named settings (such as high, medium, defrost, or roast), you'll have to use the following test. In a 4-cup measure combine 1 cup cold water and eight ice cubes. Stir for 1 minute. Pour off 1 cup of the water into a 1-cup measure and discard the ice cubes and any remaining water. Micro-cook the 1 cup water, uncovered, on the highest setting till it reaches a full boil, about 3 to 4 minutes. Check timing carefully. Then discard water and allow the cups to return to room temperature.

Repeat with fresh water and ice, using the setting you wish to test. If the water boils in about twice the time, the setting is 50% power. If the water boils in *less* than twice the time, the setting is *higher* than 50% power; if the water boils in *more* than twice the time, the setting is *lower* than 50% power.

If your microwave oven has only one setting other than 100% power, test the oven as above. If the setting is higher than 50% power, you should not use it for recipes requiring 50% power or less. If the setting is less than 50% power, use the lower setting. You may need to allow a longer cooking time.

Microwave Cookware

One of the many advantages of the microwave oven is that you often can mix, cook, and serve in one container.

Microwave-safe glass utensils and serving dishes are good choices. To make sure a dish is microwave-safe, pour ½ cup water into a glass measure. Set it inside or beside the dish you wish to test. Micro-cook on 100% power (HIGH) for 1 minute.

If the water is warm but the dish remains cool, you may use the dish for microwave cooking. If the water is warm and the dish is lukewarm, you may use the dish for heating food. If the water stays cool and the dish is hot, do not use the dish. Also do not use a dish or plate that has metallic trim or a metallic signature on the bottom.

Your owner's manual will tell you whether you can use metal in your oven. Even if you can use metal, use it only in small amounts in proportion to the amount of food because metal reflects microwave energy. Also never allow any metal to touch the sides of your microwave oven during cooking.

You can use paper products in the microwave oven, but limit the cooking time to 4 minutes (10 minutes for frozen foods). Use only white paper products for microwave cooking because dyes may bleed or may be toxic.

Most plastics, except melamine, are acceptable for microwave cooking. Because plastics vary in the food temperatures they will withstand, be sure to follow the directions from the utensil's manufacturer.

Your Microwave Wattage

Because all microwave ovens do not have the same power, check the wattage of your microwave oven. We tested our recipes in 600- to 700-watt ovens. If your oven differs, use your owner's manual as a guide.

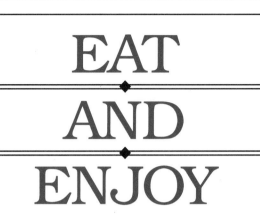

CHAPTER ONE

EAT
AND
ENJOY

Even
though you're dieting,
you still can enjoy meal-
time. With everything from
slenderizing main dishes
to guiltless desserts, you
won't have to sacrifice
flavor to reduce calories.
And to make dieting easier
than ever, these recipes
couple the speed and con-
venience of microwave
cooking with commonly
available low-calorie
ingredients.

Barbecue Beef Tortillas

339 calories/serving

A quickly made tossed salad plus these spicy tortillas make a complete meal.

1 pound beef flank steak, trimmed of separable fat
½ cup chopped onion
¼ cup chopped celery
1 tablespoon vinegar
1 teaspoon dry mustard
1 teaspoon chili powder
½ teaspoon dried basil, crushed
¼ teaspoon salt
¼ teaspoon garlic powder
2 teaspoons cornstarch
1 8-ounce can tomato sauce
1 teaspoon brown sugar
4 8-inch flour tortillas
2 tablespoons snipped chives (optional)

● Partially freeze meat. Very thinly slice across the grain into bite-size strips; set aside. In a 2-quart casserole stir together onion, celery, vinegar, dry mustard, chili powder, basil, salt, garlic powder, and 1 tablespoon *water.* Stir in meat. Micro-cook, covered, on 100% power (HIGH) for 3 minutes. Stir. Micro-cook, covered, on 50% power (MEDIUM) about 20 minutes more or till meat is tender, stirring twice.

● Stir together cornstarch and 1 tablespoon cold *water.* Stir cornstarch mixture, tomato sauce and brown sugar into the meat mixture. Micro-cook, uncovered, on 100% power (HIGH) for 3 to 4 minutes or till thickened and bubbly, stirring every minute.

● Place about ⅓ *cup* of the meat mixture in center of *each* tortilla. Roll up and place, seam side down, on a nonmetal serving platter. Spoon remaining meat mixture over tortillas. Micro-cook, uncovered, on 100% power (HIGH) for 1 to 2 minutes or till heated through, rotating plate a half-turn once. Top with snipped chives, if desired. Makes 4 servings.

Italian Beef and Vegetables

150 calories/serving

Eggplant, zucchini, and tomatoes team up with beef in this hearty combination.

1½ pounds lean boneless beef, trimmed of separable fat
1 teaspoon cooking oil
1 small eggplant (½ pound)
1 medium zucchini, thinly sliced (1 cup)
1 green pepper, cut into ½-inch strips (1 cup)
1 medium onion, sliced and separated into rings
1 medium tomato, peeled and cut into wedges
¼ cup calorie-reduced Italian salad dressing
¼ teaspoon dried basil, crushed
¼ teaspoon dried oregano, crushed
⅛ teaspoon dried thyme, crushed
1 teaspoon cornstarch

● Partially freeze the meat. Thinly slice the meat across the grain into bite-size strips; set aside. Preheat a 10-inch microwave browning dish on 100% power (HIGH) for 5 minutes. Use a heat-proof pastry brush to brush cooking oil on the bottom of the browning dish. Add the meat. Micro-cook, uncovered, on 100% power (HIGH) for 3 to 4 minutes or till the meat is done, stirring twice. Remove the meat and juices from the browning dish; set aside.

● Peel the eggplant; cut into ¾-inch cubes. In the browning dish combine eggplant, zucchini, green pepper, onion, tomato, salad dressing, basil, oregano, and thyme. Toss well to coat vegetables. Micro-cook, covered, on 100% power (HIGH) for 8 to 10 minutes or till the vegetables are just tender, stirring twice. Stir meat and juices into the vegetable mixture. Stir together cornstarch and 1 teaspoon cold *water;* stir into the meat-vegetable mixture. Micro-cook, uncovered, on 100% power (HIGH) for 4 to 5 minutes or till thickened and bubbly, stirring every minute. Makes 6 servings.

Barbecue Beef Tortillas

Meatballs with Wine Sauce

349 calories/serving

Spaghetti squash, with about 34 calories per cup, is a tasty alternative to pasta, which has about 192 calories per cup.

½ of a 2- to 3-pound spaghetti squash (halve squash lengthwise)
2 tablespoons water
1 beaten egg
1 tablespoon skim milk
2 tablespoons fine dry bread crumbs
2 tablespoons sliced green onion
2 tablespoons snipped parsley
⅛ teaspoon salt
⅛ teaspoon dried thyme, crushed
Dash pepper
½ pound lean ground beef
⅔ cup cold water
1 tablespoon cornstarch
1 teaspoon instant beef bouillon granules
1 teaspoon catsup
¼ teaspoon dried thyme, crushed
¼ cup burgundy

● Remove seeds from squash half. Place squash, cut side down, in a shallow baking dish. Sprinkle with the 2 tablespoons water. Cover with clear plastic wrap; vent by leaving a small area unsealed at the edge of the dish. Micro-cook on 100% power (HIGH) for 10 to 14 minutes or till the pulp can just be pierced with a fork, rotating the dish a half-turn twice. Let stand, covered, 10 minutes.

● Meanwhile, in a mixing bowl stir together the egg and skim milk. Stir in the bread crumbs, onion, parsley, salt, the ⅛ teaspoon dried thyme, and pepper. Add beef; mix well. Shape ground beef mixture into 8 large meatballs. In a 9-inch pie plate arrange the meatballs in a circle. Micro-cook, uncovered, on 100% power (HIGH) for 3 to 5 minutes or till the meatballs are done, rearranging meatballs and rotating the pie plate a half-turn once. Drain off liquid.

● For sauce, in a small bowl or a 2-cup measure stir together the ⅔ cup water and cornstarch. Stir in beef bouillon granules, catsup, and the ¼ teaspoon dried thyme. Micro-cook, uncovered, on 100% power (HIGH) for 2 to 3 minutes or till the sauce is thickened and bubbly, stirring every minute. Stir in the burgundy. Pour the sauce over the meatballs in the pie plate. Micro-cook, uncovered, on 100% power (HIGH) about 2 minutes or till heated through.

● Meanwhile, use a kitchen fork to shred and separate the squash pulp into strands. Pile the squash onto 2 dinner plates. Top with meatballs and sauce. Makes 2 servings.

1 Removing the spaghetti squash

Loosen the pulp of the cooked squash from the skin with a kitchen fork. Then remove the pulp by gently shredding and separating it into spaghetti-like strands.

2 Serving meatballs and sauce

To assure that this entrée will be piping hot when served, wait to micro-cook the meatballs with the sauce till just before serving. Arrange the spaghetti squash on individual dinner plates during the final heating of the meatballs and sauce. Immediately arrange meatballs atop the squash. Spoon sauce over meatballs.

1 Rolling the lasagna noodles

Spread some of the spinach-meat mixture on each lasagna noodle. Then roll up each noodle jelly-roll style, starting with one of the short edges. Place the lasagna rolls, seam side down, in a 10x6x2-inch baking dish.

2 Serving the lasagna rolls

Pour tomato-herb sauce over lasagna rolls. Micro-cook, uncovered, on 100% power (HIGH) for 10 to 12 minutes or till heated through, rotating the dish a half-turn twice. Use a wide spatula to transfer the lasagna rolls to 6 individual dinner plates. Sprinkle each roll with some of the Parmesan cheese.

Spinach-Lasagna Rolls

253 calories/serving

All the favorite flavors of classic lasagna are rolled up in easy-to-serve portions.

6 lasagna noodles
1 10-ounce package frozen chopped spinach, thawed
½ pound lean ground beef
1 medium onion, chopped
1 cup low-fat cottage cheese
1 slightly beaten egg yolk
1 teaspoon dried oregano, crushed
1 teaspoon dried basil, crushed
1 clove garlic, minced
¼ teaspoon salt
1 15-ounce can tomato-herb sauce
¼ cup grated Parmesan cheese

● Cook noodles according to package directions; drain. Thoroughly drain spinach, pressing out excess liquid. In a 1½-quart casserole micro-cook spinach, covered, on 100% power (HIGH) for 7 to 9 minutes or till done, stirring once. Drain.

● Crumble beef into a 9-inch pie plate. Stir in onion. Micro-cook, uncovered, on 100% power (HIGH) for 3 to 5 minutes or till beef is done, stirring twice to break up meat. Drain off fat.

● Stir together cottage cheese, egg yolk, oregano, basil, garlic, and salt. Stir cottage cheese mixture and meat mixture into spinach. Spread some spinach-meat mixture on each lasagna noodle. Roll up jelly-roll style, starting with one short edge. Place, seam side down, in a 10x6x2-inch baking dish. Pour tomato-herb sauce over rolls. Micro-cook, uncovered, on 100% power (HIGH) for 10 to 12 minutes or till heated through, rotating a half-turn twice. Transfer to individual plates. Sprinkle some of the Parmesan cheese on each roll. Makes 6 servings.

Veal and Spinach Roll-Ups

239 calories/serving

You'll taste a hint of horseradish in these attractive roll-ups.

1 pound boneless veal leg round steak, cut ½ inch thick and trimmed of separable fat
1 small onion, chopped
1 10-ounce package frozen chopped spinach, thawed
1 2½-ounce jar sliced mushrooms, drained
½ teaspoon prepared horseradish
¼ teaspoon salt
¼ cup shredded mozzarella cheese (1 ounce)
1 tablespoon butter *or* margarine
1½ teaspoons cornstarch
2 teaspoons lemon juice
½ teaspoon instant beef bouillon granules
¼ teaspoon Kitchen Bouquet (optional)
1 teaspoon snipped chives

● Use a meat mallet to pound steak to ¼-inch thickness. Cut into 4 serving-size pieces. In a mixing bowl stir together onion and 1 tablespoon *water*. Micro-cook, uncovered, on 100% power (HIGH) about 1 minute or till done; drain. Drain spinach, pressing out excess liquid. Stir together onion, spinach, mushrooms, horseradish, salt, and ¼ teaspoon *pepper*. Spread some spinach mixture to within ½ inch of the edge of each piece of meat. Sprinkle cheese atop. Roll up jelly-roll style, starting at one short side. Use toothpicks to secure.

● In an 8x8x2-inch baking dish micro-cook butter, uncovered, on 100% power (HIGH) for 30 to 45 seconds or till melted. Arrange veal rolls in baking dish. Turn to coat with butter. Cover with clear plastic wrap; vent by leaving a small area unsealed at the edge of the dish. Micro-cook on 50% power (MEDIUM) about 16 minutes or till meat is tender, turning and rearranging rolls once. Drain off juices, reserving ⅓ *cup*. Strain. Cover meat with foil to keep warm.

● Meanwhile, for sauce, stir together cornstarch and 1 tablespoon cold *water*. Stir in reserved ⅓ cup juices, lemon juice, and bouillon. Micro-cook, uncovered, on 100% power (HIGH) for 1 to 2 minutes or till thickened and bubbly, stirring every minute. Stir in Kitchen Bouquet, if desired. Transfer rolls to a platter; pour sauce atop. Sprinkle with chives. Makes 4 servings.

Cranberry-Apple Glazed Ham

Orange-Ginger Lamb Ring with Peas

318 calories/serving

Shaping this ground meat mixture into a ring is necessary for uniform cooking in the microwave oven.

2 beaten eggs
2 tablespoons water
½ cup quick-cooking rolled oats
1 small onion, chopped (¼ cup)
½ teaspoon salt
½ teaspoon finely shredded orange peel
  Dash pepper
1 pound ground lamb
1 10-ounce package frozen peas
1 cup frozen small whole onions
2 tablespoons water
1 tablespoon frozen orange juice concentrate
2 tablespoons orange marmalade
2 teaspoons soy sauce
¼ teaspoon ground ginger
1 11-ounce can mandarin orange sections, drained

● In a mixing bowl stir together eggs and 2 tablespoons water. Stir in oats, chopped onion, salt, orange peel, and pepper. Add lamb; mix well. Place a 6-ounce custard cup, open side up, in the center of a 9-inch pie plate. Shape the meat mixture into a ring around the custard cup. Cover with waxed paper. Micro-cook on 100% power (HIGH) for 6 to 8 minutes or till meat is done, rotating the pie plate a quarter-turn every 3 minutes. Remove custard cup. Spoon off the fat. Cover the meat with foil; set aside.

● For vegetable mixture, in a mixing bowl combine peas, small whole onions, 2 tablespoons water, and orange juice concentrate. Cover with clear plastic wrap; vent by leaving a small area unsealed at edge of the bowl. Micro-cook on 100% power (HIGH) for 5 to 7 minutes or till tender, stirring twice. Sprinkle with salt and pepper.

● Meanwhile, for the glaze, stir together orange marmalade, soy sauce, and ginger. If desired, transfer meat to a nonmetal serving platter. Spoon glaze over meat. Fill center of ring with some of the vegetable mixture. Arrange mandarin orange sections around outside and on top of meat. Cover with waxed paper. Micro-cook on 100% power (HIGH) for 1 to 2 minutes or till heated through. Pass remaining vegetable mixture. Makes 6 servings.

Cranberry-Apple Glazed Ham

172 calories/serving

Some of the cranberries pop during cooking, releasing their refreshing flavor.

1 tablespoon brown sugar
2 teaspoons cornstarch
  Dash ground allspice
½ cup low-calorie cranberry juice cocktail
1 small apple, cored and chopped (½ cup)
½ cup cranberries
1 pound fully cooked ham, sliced ⅛ inch thick

● In a 2-cup measure stir together brown sugar, cornstarch, and allspice. Stir in the cranberry juice cocktail. Add the chopped apple and cranberries; mix well. Micro-cook, uncovered, on 100% power (HIGH) for 3 to 5 minutes or till thickened and bubbly, stirring every minute. Set cranberry-apple mixture aside, covered.

● Arrange ham slices in a 12x7½x2-inch baking dish. Cover with clear plastic wrap; vent by leaving a small area unsealed at the edge of the dish. Micro-cook on 100% power (HIGH) for 3 to 4 minutes or till heated through. To serve, arrange ham slices on 4 dinner plates. Spoon cranberry-apple mixture over ham. Makes 4 servings.

Curried Pork and Tomatoes

225 calories/serving

A covering of clear plastic wrap speeds cooking in this recipe because it allows steaming as well as micro-cooking of the food. (Pictured on pages 4 and 5.)

1 pound boneless pork, trimmed of separable fat and cut into ½-inch cubes
½ cup sliced fresh mushrooms
1 small onion, chopped (¼ cup)
1 small stalk celery, thinly sliced (¼ cup)
½ of a small green pepper, chopped (¼ cup)
1 16-ounce can tomatoes, cut up
1 tablespoon cornstarch
2 teaspoons curry powder
½ teaspoon salt
½ teaspoon garlic powder
¼ teaspoon pepper
2 tablespoons snipped parsley
3 cups hot cooked rice

● In a 2-quart casserole combine pork, mushrooms, onion, celery, and green pepper. Micro-cook, covered, on 50% power (MEDIUM) for 12 to 14 minutes or till pork is no longer pink, stirring twice. Drain.

● Stir together *undrained* tomatoes, cornstarch, curry powder, salt, garlic powder, and pepper. Stir into meat mixture. Cover with clear plastic wrap; vent by leaving a small area unsealed at the edge of the casserole.

● Micro-cook on 100% power (HIGH) about 10 minutes or till thickened and bubbly, stirring every 3 minutes. Micro-cook, covered, on 100% power (HIGH) for 2 minutes more. Meanwhile, stir the parsley into the rice. Serve the meat mixture over the rice mixture. Makes 6 servings.

Orange-Sauced Chicken

216 calories/serving

A delicate combination of orange juice and garlic seasons this tasty dish. (Pictured on page 33.)

½ cup unsweetened orange juice
1½ teaspoons cornstarch
1½ teaspoons instant chicken bouillon granules
⅛ teaspoon garlic powder
2 whole large chicken breasts, skinned, halved lengthwise, and boned
Sprigs of fresh tarragon (optional)
Orange wedges (optional)

● In a 2-cup measure stir together orange juice, cornstarch, bouillon granules, and garlic powder. Micro-cook, uncovered, on 100% power (HIGH) for 2 to 4 minutes or till thickened and bubbly, stirring every minute.

● Make 3 diagonal slashes on surface of each chicken portion, if desired. Arrange chicken in a 10x6x2-inch baking dish. Pour orange juice mixture over chicken. Cover with clear plastic wrap; vent by leaving a small area unsealed at the edge of the dish. Micro-cook on 100% power (HIGH) for 5 to 7 minutes or till chicken is tender, turning chicken and rotating the dish a quarter-turn once.

● To serve, place chicken portions on 4 dinner plates. Spoon orange juice mixture atop. Garnish with fresh tarragon and orange wedges, if desired. Makes 4 servings.

Peachy Chicken

312 calories/serving

This entrée shows how well the Oriental seasonings, soy sauce and gingerroot, complement both fruit and poultry.

1 8½-ounce can calorie-reduced peach slices
   Water
1 tablespoon soy sauce
2 teaspoons cornstarch
¾ teaspoon grated gingerroot
2 whole large chicken breasts, skinned, halved lengthwise, and boned
2 cups hot cooked rice

● Drain the peach slices, reserving juice in a 2-cup measure. Add enough water to the peach juice to equal ¾ cup total liquid. Set peach slices aside. Stir soy sauce, cornstarch, and grated gingerroot into liquid. Micro-cook, uncovered, on 100% power (HIGH) for 2 to 3 minutes or till thickened and bubbly, stirring every minute.

● Arrange chicken in a 10x6x2-inch baking dish; pour peach juice mixture over chicken. Cover with clear plastic wrap; vent by leaving a small area unsealed at the edge of the dish. Micro-cook on 100% power (HIGH) for 5 to 7 minutes or till chicken is tender, turning chicken and rotating the dish a quarter-turn once. Add peach slices. Micro-cook, uncovered, on 100% power (HIGH) about 1 minute or till peaches are heated through. Serve over hot cooked rice. Makes 4 servings.

Chicken-Asparagus Pitas

169 calories/serving

One serving plus a glass of skim milk is a complete and nutritious meal.

¼ cup cold water
2 tablespoons soy sauce
5 teaspoons cornstarch
1 teaspoon vinegar
½ teaspoon dry mustard
½ teaspoon ground ginger
1 10-ounce package frozen cut asparagus
¼ cup chopped canned water chestnuts
¼ cup sliced green onion
1½ cups chopped cooked chicken
2 large pita bread rounds

● In a 1½-quart casserole stir together the cold water, soy sauce, cornstarch, vinegar, dry mustard, and ground ginger. If necessary, break up the frozen block of asparagus. Stir asparagus, chopped water chestnuts, and sliced green onion into soy sauce mixture. Micro-cook, uncovered, on 100% power (HIGH) about 5 minutes or till the asparagus is crisp-tender, stirring every 2 minutes.

● Stir in cooked chicken. Micro-cook, uncovered, on 100% power (HIGH) for 3 to 4 minutes or till chicken is heated through. Cut pita bread rounds in half crosswise. Spoon the chicken-asparagus mixture into the pita halves. Makes 4 servings.

Cranberry-Raisin Chicken

170 calories/serving

Both the sauce and stuffing offer delicious cranberry flavor.

2 whole large chicken breasts, skinned, halved lengthwise, and boned
1 slice firm-textured white bread, cut into ½-inch cubes
1 small apple, chopped (about ½ cup)
¼ cup cranberries, coarsely chopped
3 tablespoons low-calorie cranberry juice cocktail
Kitchen Bouquet (optional)
1 tablespoon brown sugar
1½ teaspoons cornstarch
⅛ teaspoon ground cinnamon
⅛ teaspoon ground nutmeg
⅓ cup low-calorie cranberry juice cocktail
¼ cup raisins

● Place one piece of chicken, boned side up, between two pieces of clear plastic wrap. Working from center to edges, pound lightly with a meat mallet, forming a rectangle about ⅛ inch thick. Remove plastic wrap. Repeat with remaining chicken.
● For stuffing, stir together bread cubes, apple, and cranberries. Add the 3 tablespoons cranberry juice cocktail; toss. Place some stuffing in center of each chicken piece. Fold two ends of each chicken piece over stuffing; secure with wooden toothpicks. Place chicken rolls, seam side down, in a 9-inch pie plate. Brush with Kitchen Bouquet, if desired. Cover with clear plastic wrap; vent by leaving a small area unsealed at edge of the dish. Micro-cook on 100% power (HIGH) for 6 to 8 minutes or till tender, rotating dish and rearranging chicken once. Let stand, covered, while preparing sauce.
● For sauce, in a 2-cup measure combine brown sugar, cornstarch, cinnamon, and nutmeg. Stir in the ⅓ cup cranberry juice cocktail. Stir in raisins. Micro-cook, uncovered, on 100% power (HIGH) for 1½ to 2 minutes or till thickened and bubbly, stirring every minute. Transfer chicken to dinner plates. Spoon sauce over chicken. Makes 4 servings.

1 Boning chicken breasts

Pull the skin away from the meat; discard. Place a chicken breast, bone side up, on a cutting board. Use a large heavy knife to split the chicken breast in half lengthwise.

Turn chicken breast half so bone side is down. Starting from the breastbone side, cut the meat away from the bones using a thin-bladed sharp knife. Press the flat side of the knife blade against the rib bones. Continue cutting, using a sawing motion. As you cut, pull the meat up and away from the bones, as shown. Repeat with remaining pieces of chicken.

2 Pounding the chicken breasts

Place one chicken breast half, boned side up, between two pieces of clear plastic wrap. Working from the center to the edges, pound lightly with the flat side of a meat mallet, forming a rectangle about ⅛ inch thick. (Use the flat side of the meat mallet to avoid tearing the meat.) Remove clear plastic wrap. Repeat with the remaining portions of chicken.

3 Serving the chicken rolls

Micro-cook the chicken first and let it stand, covered, while you prepare and cook the sauce. It's important to work quickly so the chicken does not become cool before the hot sauce is ready to be spooned over it.

Cornish Game Hen with Pineapple Brown Rice

368 calories/serving

The pineapple adds delicate flavor and moistness to the brown rice and does so with fewer calories than a rich sauce.

- 1 1- to 1½-pound frozen Cornish game hen
- 1 8-ounce can crushed pineapple (juice pack)
- ⅓ cup quick-cooking brown rice
- ½ of a small green pepper, chopped (¼ cup)
- 3 tablespoons water
- 2 teaspoons Dijon-style mustard
- ½ teaspoon dried thyme, crushed
- 1 teaspoon water (optional)
- ¼ teaspoon Kitchen Bouquet (optional)

● Thaw game hen.* Cut in half lengthwise. In a 10x6x2-inch baking dish stir together *undrained* pineapple, *uncooked* rice, green pepper, the 3 tablespoons water, mustard, and thyme. Cover with clear plastic wrap; vent by leaving a small area unsealed at the edge of the dish. Micro-cook on 100% power (HIGH) for 5 minutes.

● Place hen halves, cut side up, on rice mixture. Cover with clear plastic wrap; vent by leaving a small area unsealed at edge of the dish. Micro-cook on 100% power (HIGH) for 7 minutes. Turn hen halves cut side down. Brush skin with a mixture of the 1 teaspoon water and Kitchen Bouquet, if desired. Cover with plastic wrap; vent by leaving a small area unsealed at edge of the dish. Micro-cook on 50% power (MEDIUM) for 9 to 11 minutes or till legs move easily in sockets, rotating the dish a half-turn once. Makes 2 servings.

*Note: To thaw the Cornish game hen, place unwrapped hen, breast side down, in a 10x6x2-inch baking dish. Cover with waxed paper. Micro-cook on 50% power (MEDIUM) for 5 to 7 minutes per pound or till nearly defrosted, turning hen, breast side up, halfway through defrosting time. Let stand for 5 to 10 minutes or till completely defrosted.

Tropical Tuna Melt

249 calories/serving

Savor the flavor combination of pineapple and tuna.

- 1 8¼-ounce can crushed pineapple
- 3 tablespoons salad dressing *or* mayonnaise
- 1 teaspoon Dijon-style mustard
- 1 6½-ounce can tuna (water pack), drained and flaked
- 1 small stalk celery, thinly sliced (¼ cup)
- 2 English muffins, split and toasted
- 2 slices calorie-reduced American cheese *or* Monterey Jack cheese

● Thoroughly drain the pineapple, reserving *1 teaspoon* juice. Stir together the reserved 1 teaspoon pineapple juice, the salad dressing, and the mustard.

● In a small bowl stir together the drained pineapple, the tuna, and the celery; stir in salad dressing mixture. Arrange the toasted English muffins in an 8x8x2-inch baking dish. Top each English muffin half with some of the tuna mixture. Cut the cheese slices in half diagonally. Top each muffin half with 1 of the triangles of cheese. Micro-cook, uncovered, on 100% power (HIGH) for 1 to 2 minutes or till cheese is melted, rotating the dish a half-turn once. Makes 4 servings.

Clam-Stuffed Snapper

285 calories/serving

For your convenience, most seafood markets sell dressed fish that are eviscerated and scaled; some fish also are sold with head, fins, or tail removed.

1 2-pound fresh *or* frozen
   dressed red snapper, head
   removed
¼ cup sliced green onion
1 small stalk celery, chopped
   (¼ cup)
1 tablespoon diet margarine
1 6½-ounce can minced
   clams, drained
¾ cup plain croutons
1 tablespoon snipped parsley
2 teaspoons lemon juice
¼ teaspoon salt
⅛ teaspoon dried tarragon,
   crushed
   Dash pepper
   Lemon juice

● Thaw snapper, if frozen.* For stuffing, in a 1-quart casserole stir together green onion, celery, and margarine. Micro-cook, covered, on 100% power (HIGH) for 2 to 3 minutes or till the vegetables are just tender, stirring once. Stir in clams, croutons, parsley, 2 teaspoons lemon juice, salt, tarragon, and pepper.
● Place fish in a 12x7½x2-inch baking dish. Lightly pack stuffing into the fish cavity. Sprinkle the skin of the fish lightly with lemon juice.
● Cover with waxed paper. Micro-cook on 70% power (MEDIUM-HIGH) for 15 to 20 minutes or till fish flakes easily when tested with a fork, rotating the dish a half-turn after 8 minutes. Let stuffed fish stand, covered, about 3 minutes before serving. Makes 5 servings.
*Note: To thaw fish, in a 12x7½x2-inch baking dish micro-cook fish, uncovered, on 50% power (MEDIUM) for 3 to 5 minutes per pound or till nearly defrosted, turning fish and rotating the dish once. Let stand 5 minutes. Rinse in cool water.

Stuffing the red snapper

Before micro-cooking the red snapper, use a spoon to lightly pack the clam stuffing into the fish cavity. If you have trouble fitting all of the stuffing into the fish, use a knife to slightly enlarge the fish cavity.

Scallops in White Wine Sauce

150 calories/serving

Because the white membrane on the orange peel is bitter, use a vegetable peeler to remove the orange-colored zest only.

- 1 pound fresh *or* frozen scallops
- 1 cup sliced fresh mushrooms
- 2 teaspoons diet margarine
- 2 tablespoons orange peel cut into very fine julienne strips
- 1 tablespoon dry white wine
- 2 teaspoons cornstarch
- ¼ teaspoon salt
  Dash pepper
- 2 tablespoons cold water

● Thaw scallops, if frozen.* Quarter any large scallops. Rinse scallops in cool water; drain and set aside. In a 2-quart casserole micro-cook mushrooms and margarine, uncovered, on 100% power (HIGH) for 1 to 2 minutes or till mushrooms are tender. Stir in fresh or thawed scallops, orange peel, and wine. Micro-cook, covered, on 100% power (HIGH) for 2 to 3 minutes or till scallops are tender, stirring once. Use a slotted spoon to remove scallops and mushrooms; set aside. Reserve cooking liquid in the 2-quart casserole.

● For sauce, stir together the cornstarch, salt, and pepper. Stir in cold water. Stir the cornstarch mixture into the reserved cooking liquid. Micro-cook, uncovered, on 100% power (HIGH) for 2 to 3 minutes or till thickened and bubbly, stirring every minute. Stir scallops and mushrooms into sauce. Micro-cook, covered, on 100% power (HIGH) about 1 minute or till heated through. Makes 4 servings.

*Note: To thaw scallops, in a mixing bowl micro-cook, uncovered, on 50% power (MEDIUM) about 7 minutes or till nearly thawed, removing thawed portions twice.

Seafood Stew

158 calories/serving

For stew that's a little spicier, stir in a few dashes of bottled hot pepper sauce just before serving.

- ½ pound frozen perch fillets
- 1 10-ounce package frozen cut okra
- 1 16-ounce can tomatoes, cut up
- 2 8-ounce cans tomato sauce
- 1 medium onion, chopped
- ½ of a small green pepper, chopped (¼ cup)
- 1 clove garlic, minced
- ½ teaspoon Italian seasoning
- ¼ teaspoon instant chicken bouillon granules
- ¼ teaspoon pepper
- 1 6½-ounce can minced clams
- 1 4½-ounce can shrimp, rinsed and drained

● Thaw fillets.* Skin and cut into bite-size pieces. If necessary, break up frozen block of okra. In a 2½-quart casserole stir together okra, *undrained* tomatoes, tomato sauce, perch fillet pieces, onion, green pepper, garlic, Italian seasoning, bouillon granules, pepper, and ½ teaspoon *salt.* Micro-cook, covered, on 100% power (HIGH) for 10 to 13 minutes or till the fish flakes easily when tested with a fork and the vegetables are tender, stirring twice.

● Stir in clams and shrimp. Micro-cook, covered, on 100% power (HIGH) for 3 to 4 minutes or till heated through, stirring once. Let mixture stand, covered, for 3 minutes before serving. Makes 6 servings.

*Note: To thaw perch fillets, in a 2½-quart casserole, micro-cook, uncovered, on 50% power (MEDIUM) for 3 to 5 minutes or till nearly defrosted, separating and rearranging fillets once. Let stand 5 minutes or till completely defrosted.

Scallops in White Wine Sauce

Halibut in Vegetable Sauce

244 calories/serving

The first heating of the halibut will thaw the fish just enough so that you can cut it.

1 pound frozen halibut *or* other fish fillets
1 16-ounce can tomatoes, cut up
1 green pepper, coarsely chopped (about ¾ cup)
1 2½-ounce jar sliced mushrooms, drained
1 small onion, chopped (¼ cup)
1 tablespoon dried parsley flakes
½ teaspoon salt
½ teaspoon chili powder
¼ teaspoon garlic powder
⅛ teaspoon pepper
1 tablespoon cornstarch
1 tablespoon cold water

● To partially thaw halibut, place frozen fillets in a 10x6x2-inch baking dish. Micro-cook, uncovered, on 30% power (MEDIUM-LOW) for 8 minutes. On a cutting board crosswise cut partially thawed fillets into four portions. Return fish to the baking dish. Cover with clear plastic wrap; vent by leaving a small area unsealed at the edge of the dish. Micro-cook on 100% power (HIGH) for 6 to 8 minutes or till the fish flakes easily when tested with a fork, rotating the dish a half-turn once. Drain; cover and set aside.

● In a mixing bowl combine tomatoes, green pepper, mushrooms, onion, parsley, salt, chili powder, garlic powder, and pepper. Cover with clear plastic wrap; vent by leaving a small area unsealed at the edge of the bowl. Micro-cook on 100% power (HIGH) for 8 to 10 minutes or till green pepper is tender and sauce is bubbly, stirring every 3 minutes.

● Stir together cornstarch and water. Stir into tomato mixture. Micro-cook, covered, on 100% power (HIGH) for 2 to 3 minutes or till thickened and bubbly, stirring every minute. Micro-cook, covered, on 100% power (HIGH) for 1 minute longer. Pour tomato mixture over fish. Makes 4 servings.

Cheese Manicotti

152 calories/serving

A Test Kitchen home economist said that using a small spoon made it easy to fill the manicotti with the cheese mixture.

4 manicotti shells
1 cup low-fat cottage cheese
1 beaten egg
½ cup herb-seasoned stuffing mix
1 2-ounce can mushroom stems and pieces, drained
2 tablespoons chopped green pepper
1 tablespoon grated Parmesan cheese
1 tablespoon snipped parsley
1½ teaspoons snipped chives
½ cup tomato sauce
¼ teaspoon garlic powder
¼ teaspoon Italian seasoning
2 teaspoons snipped chives

● Cook manicotti according to package directions. Rinse with cold water. Drain and set aside. Place the cottage cheese in a food processor bowl or blender container. Cover and process till the cottage cheese is smooth. In a mixing bowl stir together the egg, stuffing mix, mushrooms, green pepper, Parmesan cheese, parsley, and the 1½ teaspoons chives. Stir in the cottage cheese. Spoon *one-fourth* of the cheese mixture into *each* manicotti shell. Place in a 10x6x2-inch baking dish.

● In a small bowl stir together the tomato sauce, garlic powder, and Italian seasoning. Pour the tomato mixture over the filled manicotti shells. Sprinkle with the 2 teaspoons chives.

● Cover the baking dish with clear plastic wrap; vent by leaving a small area unsealed at the edge of the dish. Micro-cook on 50% power (MEDIUM) for 8 to 10 minutes or till heated through. Makes 4 servings.

Ham and Egg Casserole

222 calories/serving

To ensure uniform cooking, be sure to push the cooked egg portions to the center several times during cooking.

1 6¾-ounce can chunk-style ham, drained and flaked
1 4-ounce can sliced mushrooms, drained
6 beaten eggs
⅓ cup skim milk
2 tablespoons grated Parmesan cheese
1 teaspoon dried parsley flakes
½ teaspoon onion powder
⅛ teaspoon pepper
1 cup shredded mozzarella cheese (4 ounces)

● In a 1½-quart casserole stir together the ham and the drained mushrooms. In a mixing bowl stir together the eggs, skim milk, grated Parmesan cheese, dried parsley flakes, onion powder, and pepper.

● Pour the egg mixture evenly over the ham mixture in the casserole. Micro-cook, uncovered, on 100% power (HIGH) for 4 to 6 minutes or till the egg mixture is almost set, pushing cooked portions to center of the casserole several times during cooking. Sprinkle with the shredded mozzarella cheese. Let stand for 5 minutes. Makes 6 servings.

Cooking Egg Mixtures in the Microwave Oven

To avoid forming tough portions in an egg mixture, thoroughly beat together the egg yolk and egg white before cooking recipes such as Ham and Egg Casserole in the microwave oven.

If the yolk and white are not thoroughly beaten together, the yolk portions of the mixture will cook faster and become tough before the white portions are done.

Pizza Eggs

Pizza Eggs

225 calories/serving

Italian seasoning and pizza sauce give this egg dish all the zesty flavor of pizza with just a fraction of the calories.

1 tablespoon diet margarine
1 small onion, chopped (¼ cup)
½ of a small green pepper, chopped (¼ cup)
8 beaten eggs
½ cup skim milk
1 2½-ounce jar sliced mushrooms, drained
½ teaspoon salt
½ teaspoon Italian seasoning (optional)
¼ teaspoon pepper
½ cup pizza sauce
¼ cup shredded mozzarella cheese (1 ounce)
2 ripe olives, sliced (optional)
  Cilantro (optional)

● In an 8x1½-inch round baking dish micro-cook margarine, uncovered, on 100% power (HIGH) for 30 to 45 seconds or till melted. Add onion and green pepper. Micro-cook, uncovered, on 100% power (HIGH) for 2 to 3 minutes or till vegetables are tender. Combine eggs; milk; mushrooms; salt; Italian seasoning, if desired; and pepper; pour into baking dish. Micro-cook, uncovered, on 100% power (HIGH) for 5 to 6 minutes or till eggs are almost set, pushing cooked portions to center of dish several times during cooking.
● Pour pizza sauce over eggs. Sprinkle with mozzarella cheese. Micro-cook, uncovered, on 100% power (HIGH) for 1 to 2 minutes or till cheese starts to melt. If desired, garnish with sliced olives and cilantro. Cut into wedges to serve. Makes 4 servings.

Crab Puff

252 calories/serving

This delicate puff falls quickly. So make sure everyone is ready to eat as soon as it finishes cooking.

¼ cup diet margarine
¼ cup all-purpose flour
2 tablespoons snipped parsley
½ teaspoon dry mustard
⅛ teaspoon paprika
  Dash pepper
1 cup skim milk
6 slices calorie-reduced Monterey Jack cheese, torn up (4 ounces)
3 egg yolks
1 7-ounce can crab meat, drained, flaked, and cartilage removed
3 egg whites
¼ teaspoon cream of tartar

● In a 2-quart mixing bowl micro-cook margarine, uncovered, on 100% power (HIGH) about 1 minute or till melted. Stir in flour, parsley, mustard, paprika, and pepper. Stir in milk. Micro-cook, uncovered, on 100% power (HIGH) for 3 to 4 minutes or till thickened and bubbly, stirring every minute. Micro-cook, uncovered, on 100% power (HIGH) for 1 minute more. Stir in cheese till melted. Beat egg yolks with fork. Gradually add about *1 cup* of the hot mixture to egg yolks. Return to mixing bowl. Stir in the flaked crab.
● In a large mixer bowl beat egg whites and cream of tartar till stiff peaks form (tips stand straight). Gently fold into crab mixture. Pour into an ungreased 6- or 6½-cup nonmetal ring mold. Micro-cook, uncovered, on 50% power (MEDIUM) for 10 to 12 minutes or till just set in center, rotating the dish a half-turn every 3 minutes. Serve immediately. Makes 4 servings.

Broccoli and Onions with Cheese Sauce

67 calories/serving

Measure the Neufchâtel cheese by dividing an 8-ounce package in quarters and slicing off three-fourths of one quarter.

1 10-ounce package frozen cut broccoli
1 medium onion, cut into thin wedges
2 tablespoons water
½ cup skim milk
1½ ounces Neufchâtel cheese, softened
1 teaspoon cornstarch
½ teaspoon lemon juice
¼ teaspoon dried basil, crushed
⅛ teaspoon dried rosemary, crushed

● In a 1½-quart casserole combine broccoli, onion, and water. Micro-cook, covered, on 100% power (HIGH) for 4 to 7 minutes or till broccoli is tender, stirring every 3 minutes. Drain broccoli and onion mixture well.

● Meanwhile, in a small bowl combine skim milk, Neufchâtel cheese, cornstarch, lemon juice, basil, and rosemary with a wire whisk. Micro-cook, uncovered, on 100% power (HIGH) for 2 to 3 minutes or till thickened and bubbly, stirring every minute. Pour cheese mixture over vegetables. Makes 4 servings.

Asparagus with Herb Sauce

38 calories/serving

If you're lucky enough to have fresh thyme, snip and use ¾ teaspoon of it in this sauce instead of the dried thyme.

1 10-ounce package frozen cut asparagus
2 tablespoons water
½ cup skim milk
1 teaspoon cornstarch
¼ teaspoon dried thyme, crushed
⅛ teaspoon pepper
2 slices calorie-reduced Swiss cheese, torn up

● In a 1-quart casserole combine asparagus and water. Micro-cook, covered, on 100% power (HIGH) for 5 to 7 minutes or till tender, stirring once. Drain. Set aside, covered.

● For sauce, in a 2-cup measure stir together skim milk, cornstarch, thyme, and pepper. Micro-cook, uncovered, on 50% power (MEDIUM) for 4 to 5 minutes or till thickened and bubbly, stirring every minute. Stir in cheese. Micro-cook, uncovered, on 100% power (HIGH) for 15 to 30 seconds or till melted. Pour sauce over asparagus. Makes 4 servings.

Orange-Sauced Carrots

76 calories/serving

Use the smallest holes on your grater to prepare the finely shredded orange peel.

1 **pound carrots**
¼ **cup water**
½ **cup orange juice**
2 **teaspoons cornstarch**
1½ **teaspoons brown sugar**
¼ **teaspoon finely shredded orange peel**
¼ **teaspoon ground cinnamon**
Dash ground cloves

● Cut carrots in half crosswise. Quarter each carrot half lengthwise. In a 1-quart casserole combine carrot pieces and water. Micro-cook, covered, on 100% power (HIGH) for 8 to 10 minutes or till the carrots are tender, stirring once. Let carrots stand, covered, for 3 minutes.

● Meanwhile, in a 2-cup measure combine the orange juice and the cornstarch. Stir in the brown sugar, finely shredded orange peel, ground cinnamon, and ground cloves. Micro-cook, uncovered, on 100% power (HIGH) about 2 minutes or till the mixture is thickened and bubbly, stirring every minute. Drain the carrots. Pour the orange juice mixture over the carrots; toss to coat well. Makes 4 servings.

Spinach with Horseradish-Cucumber Sauce

63 calories/serving

Make a cucumber twist by cutting halfway across a thin slice of cucumber. Twist the ends of the slice in opposite directions.

2 **10-ounce packages frozen chopped spinach**
½ **cup calorie-reduced cucumber salad dressing**
1 **teaspoon prepared horseradish**
Cucumber twists (optional)

● In a 2-quart casserole micro-cook the frozen spinach, covered, on 100% power (HIGH) for 9 to 11 minutes or till spinach is done, stirring once. Drain the spinach thoroughly, pressing out excess liquid.

● In a small bowl combine cucumber dressing and horseradish. Stir into spinach. Micro-cook, covered, on 50% power (MEDIUM) for 1 to 3 minutes or till heated through. Garnish with cucumber twists, if desired. Makes 6 servings.

Piping Vegetable Purees

● Purees are smooth-consistency pastes made from vegetables or fruits. Smooth purees that are thick enough to mound lend themselves well to piping.

● To pipe, spoon a small amount of the chilled vegetable mixture into a pastry bag fitted with a large star tip. Hold the bag at a 90-degree angle above each plate. Squeeze about ¼ cup of the puree onto the plate. Stop pressure and lift off. Clean the pastry bag and tip well between piping different purees.

● To reheat the piped mounds, allow 30 seconds on 100% power (HIGH) for 1 mound or 45 to 60 seconds for 3 mounds.

Green Pea Puree

53 calories/serving

Pipe Parsnip Puree, Minted Carrot Puree (see recipes page 34), and Green Pea Puree into a cluster of blossoms.

1   10-ounce package frozen
    peas
2   tablespoons water
1   tablespoon skim milk
¼   teaspoon dried chervil,
    crushed
    Salt
    Pepper

● In a 1-quart casserole combine peas and water. Micro-cook, covered, on 100% power (HIGH) about 5 minutes or till done, stirring once. Drain the peas.

● In a food processor bowl or blender container combine the peas, milk, and chervil. Cover and process till the pea skins are blended and the mixture is smooth. Add salt and pepper to taste; blend till combined.

● Return the pureed mixture to the 1-quart casserole. Micro-cook, uncovered, on 100% power (HIGH) for 2 to 3 minutes or till the pureed mixture is thick enough to mound, stirring every minute. Spoon onto 4 dinner plates. (To pipe the mixture, cover and chill it till just before serving. Put the chilled mixture into a pastry bag; pipe onto 4 plates. To reheat each serving, micro-cook, uncovered, on 100% power (HIGH) about 30 seconds or till heated through.) Makes 4 servings.

Green Pea Puree

Parsnip Puree
(see recipe, page 34)

Minted Carrot Puree
(see recipe, page 34)

Orange-Sauced Chicken
(see recipe, page 18)

Parsnip Puree

53 calories/serving

Parsnip Puree, seasoned with nutmeg, has the smooth appearance of mashed potatoes. (Pictured on page 33.)

  2 **cups peeled and thinly sliced parsnips (about ⅔ pound)**
  2 **tablespoons water**
  3 **tablespoons skim milk**
  ⅛ **teaspoon salt**
     Dash ground nutmeg

● In a 1-quart casserole combine parsnips and water. Micro-cook, covered, on 100% power (HIGH) for 5 to 7 minutes or till tender; drain well. In a food processor bowl or blender container combine the parsnips, milk, salt, and nutmeg. Cover and process till smooth.

● To spoon mixture, return the parsnip mixture to the same casserole. Micro-cook, uncovered, on 100% power (HIGH) about 45 seconds or till heated through. Spoon onto 4 plates. (To pipe the mixture, cover and chill it till just before serving. Put the chilled mixture into a pastry bag; pipe onto 4 plates. To reheat each serving, micro-cook, uncovered, on 100% power (HIGH) about 30 seconds or till heated through.) Makes 4 servings.

Minted Carrot Puree

32 calories/serving

If you like, substitute fresh or dried basil for the mint. (Pictured on page 33.)

  4 **medium carrots, peeled and thinly sliced (2 cups)**
  2 **tablespoons water**
  4 **teaspoons skim milk**
  ½ **teaspoon snipped fresh mint *or* ⅛ teaspoon dried mint, crushed**
  ⅛ **teaspoon salt**

● In a 1-quart casserole combine carrots and water. Micro-cook, covered, on 100% power (HIGH) for 8 to 10 minutes or till very tender, stirring once. Drain well. In a food processor bowl or blender container combine the carrots, milk, mint, and salt. Cover and process till smooth.

● To spoon mixture, return the carrot mixture to the same casserole. Micro-cook, uncovered, on 100% power (HIGH) about 45 seconds or till heated through. Spoon onto 4 plates. (To pipe the mixture, cover and chill it till just before serving. Put the chilled mixture into a pastry bag; pipe onto 4 plates. To reheat each serving, micro-cook, uncovered, on 100% power (HIGH) about 30 seconds or till heated through.) Makes 4 servings.

Dilled Vegetable Medley

38 calories/serving

Yogurt and lemon peel add a pleasant tang to the dill flavor.

  1 **cup cauliflower flowerets**
  1 **cup sliced carrots**
  ½ **of a small cucumber, seeded and coarsely chopped**
  ½ **cup plain low-fat yogurt**
  ¼ **teaspoon dried dillweed**
  ⅛ **teaspoon finely shredded lemon peel**

● In a 1½-quart casserole combine cauliflower, carrots, cucumber, and 2 tablespoons *water*. Micro-cook, covered, on 100% power (HIGH) for 5 to 7 minutes or till crisp-tender, stirring once. Drain.

● Meanwhile, in a small mixing bowl stir together the yogurt, dillweed, lemon peel, and ¼ teaspoon *salt*; stir into cooked vegetables. Serve immediately. Makes 4 servings.

Lemon-Garlic Vegetables

33 calories/serving

Diet margarine adds a buttery flavor to the cauliflower and broccoli that's calorie-affordable.

1 10-ounce package frozen cauliflower
1 10-ounce package frozen cut broccoli
½ cup chopped sweet red pepper *or* 2 tablespoons chopped pimiento
3 tablespoons water
2 tablespoons diet margarine
1 tablespoon lemon juice
¼ teaspoon garlic powder

● In a 2-quart casserole combine cauliflower, broccoli, sweet red pepper or pimiento, and water. Micro-cook, covered, on 100% power (HIGH) for 7 to 9 minutes or till vegetables are crisp-tender, stirring twice. Let vegetables stand, covered, for 2 minutes. Drain.

● Meanwhile, in a 1-cup measure micro-cook diet margarine, uncovered, on 100% power (HIGH) for 30 to 45 seconds or till melted. Stir in lemon juice and garlic powder. Pour lemon-garlic mixture over vegetables. Makes 8 servings.

Lima Beans with Pimiento

90 calories/serving

Because lima beans are a starchy vegetable, this recipe has a few more calories than some of the others.

1 10-ounce package frozen baby lima beans
¼ cup water
2 tablespoons sliced green onion
⅛ teaspoon dried basil, crushed
⅛ teaspoon dried rosemary, crushed
Dash salt
1 2-ounce can sliced pimiento, drained and chopped
1 tablespoon diet margarine
1 tablespoon lemon juice

● In a 1½-quart casserole combine lima beans, water, green onion, basil, rosemary, and salt. Micro-cook, covered, on 100% power (HIGH) for 9 to 11 minutes or till vegetables are done, stirring 3 or 4 times. *Do not drain.*

● Stir in pimiento, diet margarine, and lemon juice. Micro-cook, covered, on 100% power (HIGH) about 1 minute or till heated through. Makes 4 servings.

Harvest Cinnamon Beans

Harvest Cinnamon Beans

44 calories/serving

You can use either fresh or frozen green beans for this tomato-flavored side dish.

1½ pounds fresh green beans, cut into 1-inch pieces, *or* two 9-ounce packages frozen cut green beans, thawed
½ cup water
1 small onion, coarsely chopped (¼ cup)
½ teaspoon instant chicken bouillon granules
¼ teaspoon ground cinnamon
2 tablespoons tomato paste
Dash pepper
Green onion fan (optional)

● Thaw green beans, if frozen.* In a 2-quart casserole combine fresh or thawed green beans, water, onion, bouillon granules, and cinnamon. Micro-cook, uncovered, on 100% power (HIGH) till beans are crisp-tender (15 to 20 minutes for fresh beans or 10 to 12 minutes for thawed beans), stirring 2 or 3 times during cooking.

● Drain bean mixture, reserving 1 teaspoon of the liquid. Combine the reserved liquid, tomato paste, and pepper. Stir tomato paste mixture into bean mixture. If desired, garnish with green onion fan. Makes 6 servings.

*Note: To thaw frozen green beans, in a 2-quart casserole micro-cook beans, uncovered, on 30% power (LOW) for 7 to 9 minutes or till beans are thawed.

Tangy Green Beans

64 calories/serving

The pickle relish and salad dressing produce a well-balanced sweet-and-sour flavor.

1 9-ounce package frozen cut green beans
2 tablespoons water
⅓ cup calorie-reduced Russian salad dressing
2 tablespoons chopped green onion
2 tablespoons chopped sweet red *or* green pepper
1 tablespoon sweet pickle relish

● In a 1-quart casserole combine beans and water. Micro-cook, covered, on 100% power (HIGH) for 5 to 6 minutes or till nearly tender, stirring once to separate beans. Drain. Let stand, covered, for 2 minutes.

● Meanwhile, stir together salad dressing, green onion, sweet red or green pepper, and pickle relish. Stir into beans. Micro-cook, covered, on 100% power (HIGH) for 2 to 3 minutes or till beans are tender. Makes 4 servings.

Vanilla Pears

151 calories/serving

Use the creamy cheese topper to dress up other fruits such as baked apples or canned peaches.

½ cup apple juice
1 teaspoon vanilla
4 pears
  Lemon juice
2 ounces Neufchâtel cheese,
  softened
½ teaspoon vanilla

● In a 1½-quart casserole combine apple juice and the 1 teaspoon vanilla. Micro-cook, covered, on 100% power (HIGH) for 2 to 3 minutes or till the mixture boils. Meanwhile, peel the pears, leaving stems intact. Insert an apple corer into the blossom end of each pear and carefully remove core. Brush the pears with lemon juice.

● Arrange fruit upright in casserole. Spoon apple juice mixture over pears. Micro-cook, covered, on 100% power (HIGH) for 6 to 10 minutes or till pears are fork-tender, rotating dish and basting with cooking liquid every 3 minutes. Cover and chill fruit in cooking liquid.

● At serving time, drain pears; reserve liquid. For topper, in a small bowl stir together Neufchâtel cheese, the ½ teaspoon vanilla, and enough of the reserved cooking liquid (about 4 teaspoons) to make a topper of desired consistency. Serve some of the topper over each pear. Makes 4 servings.

Strawberries and Cheese

129 calories/serving

This fix-ahead dessert hints of cheesecake.

4 ounces Neufchâtel cheese
½ cup skim milk
3 tablespoons sugar
1 egg yolk
½ teaspoon vanilla
1 quart fresh strawberries,
  sliced (4 cups)

● In a food processor bowl or blender container combine cheese, skim milk, sugar, and egg yolk; cover and process till smooth. Transfer mixture to a 2-cup measure. Micro-cook, uncovered, on 50% power (MEDIUM) for 4 to 5 minutes or till bubbly, stirring every minute. Stir in vanilla. Cover and chill at least two hours.

● Divide strawberries among 6 dessert dishes. Serve cheese mixture over berries. Makes 6 servings.

Vanilla Pears

Cantaberry Boats

58 calories/serving

Serve this berry-filled melon for dessert or for brunch.

⅔ cup fresh *or* frozen
    unsweetened berries
1 cantaloupe
¾ teaspoon unflavored gelatin
⅓ cup apple juice

● Thaw the berries, if frozen.* If using fresh strawberries, remove the stems and caps; cut into halves. Halve and seed the cantaloupe. Spoon *half* of the berries into the center of *each* cantaloupe half. Set aside.

● In a 2-cup measure sprinkle gelatin over apple juice. Let stand for 5 minutes. Micro-cook, uncovered, on 100% power (HIGH) about 1 minute or till the gelatin dissolves, stirring once. Pour gelatin mixture over berries in cantaloupe. Chill for several hours or overnight till firm. Cut fruit-filled cantaloupe halves in half lengthwise. Makes 4 servings.

*Note: To thaw frozen berries, in a 1-quart casserole micro-cook berries, uncovered, on 30% power (LOW) for 1½ to 2½ minutes or till nearly thawed.

Spiced Apple Flambé

151 calories/serving

A long fireplace match makes lighting the rum easier.

2 medium cooking apples,
    peeled, cored, and sliced
    ¼ inch thick
2 teaspoons lemon juice
1½ teaspoons brown sugar
1 teaspoon cornstarch
⅛ teaspoon ground cinnamon
    Dash ground cloves
¼ cup orange juice
5 teaspoons light rum

● Place apple slices in a 1-quart casserole. Brush apples with lemon juice. Set aside. In a 1-cup measure stir together brown sugar, cornstarch, cinnamon, and ground cloves. Stir in the orange juice. Micro-cook, uncovered, on 100% power (HIGH) for 1 to 2 minutes or till the mixture is thickened and bubbly, stirring once.

● Pour orange juice mixture over apples in the casserole. Micro-cook, covered, on 100% power (HIGH) about 4 minutes or till apple slices are tender, stirring once. Spoon apple mixture into 2 individual dessert dishes.

● In a 1-cup measure micro-cook the rum, uncovered, on 100% power (HIGH) for 30 seconds. Carefully ignite the rum and pour over apple mixture. Makes 2 servings.

1 Making Cantaberry Boats

Place the blueberries, strawberries, or raspberries in the center of each cantaloupe half. In a 2-cup measure sprinkle the gelatin over the apple juice. Let the mixture stand for 5 minutes to allow the gelatin to soften. Micro-cook, uncovered, on 100% power (HIGH) about 1 minute or till the gelatin is dissolved, stirring once. Pour the gelatin-apple juice mixture over the berries.

2 Serving Cantaberry Boats

Chill the Cantaberry Boats in the refrigerator for several hours or overnight till the gelatin mixture is firm. Just before serving, use a large knife to slice each berry-filled cantaloupe half in half lengthwise. The firm gelatin-apple juice mixture will hold the berries atop each cantaloupe wedge.

Glazed Citrus Sections

127 calories/serving

For variety, you may want to substitute pineapple chunks for the mandarin orange sections the next time you prepare this.

1   medium grapefruit, halved
1   11-ounce can mandarin
    orange sections, drained
1   tablespoon brown sugar
1½   teaspoons sugar
1   teaspoon rum
1   teaspoon light corn syrup
⅛   teaspoon ground cinnamon
⅛   teaspoon ground nutmeg
    Dash ground cloves

● Section grapefruit halves, leaving outside shells intact. Discard the membrane. Reserve the grapefruit shells. In a small bowl toss together grapefruit sections and mandarin orange sections. Mound the fruit into the reserved grapefruit shells. Place in a 9-inch pie plate.
● In a 1-cup measure stir together the brown sugar, sugar, rum, corn syrup, cinnamon, nutmeg, and cloves. Spoon over the fruit in the grapefruit shells.
● Micro-cook, uncovered, on 100% power (HIGH) for 2½ to 3 minutes or till the fruit is heated through, rotating dish a half-turn twice. Makes 2 servings.

Cocoa Mint Mousse

64 calories/serving

By gradually combining the hot mixture and the egg yolk, you can prevent the hot mixture from cooking the egg yolk before the two are thoroughly mixed.

1½   teaspoons unflavored
    gelatin
1¼   cups water
1   envelope sugar-free instant
    cocoa mix
1   slightly beaten egg yolk
½   teaspoon mint extract
1   8-ounce container frozen
    whipped dessert topping,
    thawed

● In a 4-cup measure sprinkle the gelatin over the water. Let stand for 5 minutes. Micro-cook, uncovered, on 100% power (HIGH) about 2 minutes or till gelatin dissolves, stirring once. Stir in cocoa mix till dissolved.
● Stir a small amount of cocoa mixture into egg yolk; return egg mixture to remaining cocoa mixture. Micro-cook, uncovered, on 100% power (HIGH) for 2 to 3 minutes or till the mixture is slightly thickened, stirring twice.
● Use a wire whisk to stir in the mint extract. Chill till the mixture is the consistency of unbeaten egg whites (partially set). Fold in the whipped dessert topping. Spoon into 8 individual dessert dishes or custard cups. Chill for several hours or overnight. Makes 8 servings.

1 Sectioning grapefruit halves

To make sectioning easy, use a grapefruit knife (a small knife with serrated edges and curved blade) to cut around the outside of the grapefruit next to the peel.

Cut to the center of the fruit between one section and the membrane. Turn the knife and cut down the other side of the section next to the membrane. Use the grapefruit knife to gently lift out each section as shown.

After all of the grapefruit sections have been removed, cut out the membrane and discard it.

2 Micro-cooking Glazed Citrus Sections

Place the fruit-filled grapefruit shells in a 9-inch pie plate. Use a large spoon to pour the sugar-rum mixture over the fruit. Micro-cook, uncovered, on 100% power (HIGH) for 2½ to 3 minutes or till the fruit is heated through.

Spiced Citrus Warmer

Harvest-of-Fruit Parfaits

Harvest-of-Fruit Parfaits

100 calories/serving

Allow 45 minutes to 1 hour for the gelatin mixture to chill until partially set and at least 3 to 4 hours for it to chill until firm.

1 cup frozen whole
    unsweetened
    strawberries
¾ cup frozen blueberries
¼ cup sugar
1½ teaspoons unflavored
    gelatin
1 11-ounce can mandarin
    orange sections
1 teaspoon finely shredded
    orange peel (set aside)
    Orange juice
1 cup halved and seeded
    grapes
    Whole strawberries
    (optional)
    Fresh mint sprigs (optional)

● Thaw strawberries and blueberries.* Cut strawberries in half. Set berries aside. In a small bowl stir together sugar and gelatin. Drain mandarin oranges, reserving juice in a 4-cup measure. Set mandarin oranges aside. Add enough orange juice to reserved juice to measure 1 cup total liquid. Stir in sugar-gelatin mixture and shredded orange peel.

● Micro-cook the gelatin mixture, uncovered, on 100% power (HIGH) for 2 to 3 minutes or till the gelatin is dissolved, stirring once. Chill till the gelatin mixture is partially set (the consistency of unbeaten egg whites).

● In each of 6 parfait glasses place blueberries, followed by halved strawberries. Pour *half* of the gelatin mixture over strawberries. Top with grapes and orange sections. Pour remaining gelatin mixture over oranges. Chill for several hours or overnight till firm. Garnish with whole strawberries and fresh mint sprigs, if desired. Makes 6 servings.

*Note: To thaw strawberries and blueberries, in a small mixing bowl micro-cook frozen berries, uncovered, on 30% power (LOW) for 1½ to 2½ minutes or till nearly thawed, rotating the dish a half-turn once.

Spiced Citrus Warmer

84 calories/serving

The lower power setting and the longer cooking time are needed to bring out the flavors of the spices.

2 cups unsweetened orange
    juice
1 cup low-calorie cranberry
    juice cocktail
½ cup water
1 tablespoon honey
3 inches stick cinnamon,
    broken
½ teaspoon whole allspice
½ teaspoon whole cloves
    Orange wedges (optional)
    Cinnamon sticks (optional)

● In a 4-cup measure stir together orange juice, cranberry juice cocktail, water, honey, 3 inches stick cinnamon, whole allspice, and whole cloves.

● Micro-cook, covered, on 100% power (HIGH) for 8 to 10 minutes or just till boiling. Continue to micro-cook, covered, on 50% power (MEDIUM) for 5 minutes. Strain to remove spices. Pour into 4 heat-proof mugs. Garnish with orange wedges and additional cinnamon sticks, if desired. Makes 4 (7-ounce) servings.

Savory Vegetable Drink

32 calories/serving

The flavor of this hot vegetable juice drink with its pleasant herb seasonings will remind you of sipping a hot soup.

1 24-ounce can vegetable juice
   cocktail
1 teaspoon Worcestershire
   sauce
¼ teaspoon dried marjoram,
   crushed
¼ teaspoon dried thyme,
   crushed
4 stalks celery (optional)

● In a 4-cup measure stir together vegetable juice cocktail, Worcestershire sauce, dried marjoram, and dried thyme. Micro-cook, covered, on 100% power (HIGH) for 5 to 6 minutes or till heated through. Pour into 4 heat-proof mugs. Serve with celery stalk stirrers, if desired. Makes 4 (6-ounce) servings.

Hot Broccoli Dip

23 calories/tablespoon

If you'd like your dip to be thinner, stir in another tablespoon of skim milk.

1 cup chopped broccoli
½ of a small onion, chopped
   (¼ cup)
2 tablespoons water
1 tablespoon lemon juice
½ teaspoon prepared
   horseradish
¼ teaspoon salt
   Dash pepper
½ of an 8-ounce package
   Neufchâtel cheese,
   softened
1 tablespoon skim milk
   Few dashes bottled hot
   pepper sauce
   Raw vegetable dippers

● In a 1-quart casserole combine broccoli, onion, and water. Micro-cook, covered, on 100% power (HIGH) for 4 to 5 minutes or till broccoli is tender. In a blender container or food processor bowl combine cooked broccoli mixture, lemon juice, horseradish, salt, and pepper. Cover and blend till smooth.
● In the 1-quart casserole gradually stir broccoli mixture into the softened cheese. Stir in the milk and hot pepper sauce. Micro-cook, uncovered, on 100% power (HIGH) about 2 minutes or till heated through, stirring once. Serve with vegetable dippers. Makes 16 (1-tablespoon) servings.

CHAPTER TWO

CALORIE-
REDUCED
CLASSICS

Now you
can eat some of the foods
you thought were too sinful
for a diet! We've selected
several favorite classic recipes
and reduced the calories
by at least 20%—sometimes
we've even halved the
calories! How did we do it?
We started with the classic
recipes. Then we began
omitting, reducing, or sub-
stituting the calorie-laden
ingredients. From there
we tested and tasted our
lighter versions to ensure
that you'd be delighted
with the results.

Vegetable-Beef Stew

234 calories/serving

Longer cooking times at lower power settings tenderize less expensive cuts of meat, such as beef chuck.

1½ pounds boneless beef chuck
2 medium onions
3 stalks celery, sliced
2 cloves garlic, minced
1 bay leaf
1 tablespoon instant beef bouillon granules
1 teaspoon dried thyme, crushed
½ teaspoon sugar
⅛ teaspoon pepper
4 medium carrots, sliced
1 8-ounce can tomato sauce
2 medium zucchini, halved lengthwise and sliced
½ of a small green pepper, chopped (¼ cup)
2 tablespoons cornstarch

● Trim meat of separable fat and cut into ¾-inch cubes. Cut onions into eighths. In a 3-quart casserole stir together beef, onions, celery, garlic, bay leaf, bouillon granules, thyme, sugar, pepper, and 1½ cups *water.* Micro-cook, covered, on 100% power (HIGH) for 5 minutes; stir. Micro-cook, covered, on 50% power (MEDIUM) for 20 minutes, stirring once.

● Stir in carrots and tomato sauce. Micro-cook, covered, on 50% power (MEDIUM) for 20 minutes, stirring once. Stir in zucchini and green pepper. Micro-cook, covered, on 50% power (MEDIUM) for 15 to 20 minutes or till meat is done and vegetables are tender, stirring every 5 minutes.

● Stir together the cornstarch and 2 tablespoons cold *water.* Stir into the meat mixture. Micro-cook, uncovered, on 100% power (HIGH) for 2 to 3 minutes or till meat mixture is thickened and bubbly, stirring every minute. Micro-cook, uncovered, on 50% power (HIGH) for 2 minutes more, stirring mixture every minute. Remove the bay leaf. Makes 8 servings.

Yogurt Beef Stroganoff

366 calories/serving

Yogurt makes this diet version tangier than the classic recipe.

¾ pound beef sirloin, trimmed of separable fat
1 teaspoon cooking oil
2 cups wide noodles
1½ cups sliced fresh mushrooms
1 medium onion, cut into thin wedges
¼ cup water
2 cloves garlic, minced
½ cup water
1 tablespoon tomato paste
1½ teaspoons instant beef bouillon granules
½ teaspoon dried dillweed *or* basil, crushed (optional)
1 8-ounce carton plain low-fat yogurt
3 tablespoons all-purpose flour

● Partially freeze beef. Thinly slice across grain into bite-size strips. Preheat a 10-inch microwave browning dish on 100% power (HIGH) for 5 minutes. Use a heat-proof pastry brush to brush cooking oil on the bottom of the browning dish. Add beef. Micro-cook, covered, on 100% power (HIGH) for 2 to 3 minutes or till done, stirring twice. Transfer meat and juices to a mixing bowl; set aside.

● Cook noodles according to package directions. Drain and set aside. Meanwhile, in the browning dish stir together the mushrooms, onion, the ¼ cup water, and garlic. Micro-cook, covered, on 100% power (HIGH) for 4 to 5 minutes or till tender, stirring once; *do not drain.* Stir the ½ cup water, tomato paste, bouillon granules, and the dillweed or basil, if desired, into mushroom mixture. Stir together yogurt and flour till smooth.

● Stir yogurt mixture into mushroom mixture. Micro-cook, uncovered, on 100% power (HIGH) for 4 to 5 minutes or till thickened and bubbly, stirring every minute. Stir in reserved meat and juices. Micro-cook, uncovered, on 100% power (HIGH) for 2 to 3 minutes or till heated through. Serve over hot cooked noodles. Makes 4 servings.

Vegetable-Beef Stew

Here's how to prepare pastitsio, a tasty main dish from Greece.

1 Preparing the pastitsio in the ring mold

Using a ring mold allows more uniform micro-cooking of the pastitsio; the outside edges do not become overdone while the center remains uncooked.

Evenly distribute the meat mixture in a 6- or 6½-cup nonmetal ring mold. Combine the ingredients for the topping in a 4-cup measure. Pour the hot topping over the meat mixture. Sprinkle cinnamon atop pastitsio for added color and flavor.

2 Serving Beef Pastitsio

Take the pastitsio out of the microwave oven when the topping is set near the outside edge but still soft near the center. The pastitsio will continue to cook during the 10 minutes of standing time. To serve, spoon the pastitsio onto individual dinner plates.

Beef Pastitsio

191 calories/serving

Although ground lamb is traditional in pastitsio, ground beef also will work well and is more readily available.

1 cup elbow macaroni
¾ pound lean ground beef *or* lean ground lamb
1 medium onion, chopped
1 8-ounce can tomato sauce
2 tablespoons grated Parmesan cheese
½ teaspoon dried thyme, crushed
¼ teaspoon salt
¼ teaspoon ground cinnamon
¾ cup skim milk
2 tablespoons cornstarch
¼ teaspoon salt
2 slightly beaten eggs
2 tablespoons grated Parmesan cheese
Ground cinnamon

● Cook macaroni according to package directions. Drain and set aside. Meanwhile, crumble beef or lamb into a 1½-quart casserole; stir in onion. Micro-cook, uncovered, on 100% power (HIGH) for 4 to 5 minutes or till meat is done and onion is tender, stirring once to break up meat. Drain off fat. Stir in the cooked elbow macaroni, tomato sauce, 2 tablespoons Parmesan cheese, thyme, ¼ teaspoon salt, and the ¼ teaspoon cinnamon. Spread the meat mixture in the bottom of a 6- or 6½-cup non-metal ring mold.

● For topping, in a 4-cup measure stir together skim milk, cornstarch, and ¼ teaspoon salt. Micro-cook, uncovered, on 100% power (HIGH) for 2 to 3 minutes or till thickened and bubbly, stirring every minute. Gradually stir about ½ cup of the hot mixture into the eggs. Return all to the 4-cup measure. Stir in 2 tablespoons grated Parmesan cheese. Pour atop meat mixture. Sprinkle with additional cinnamon. Micro-cook, uncovered, on 100% power (HIGH) for 9 to 11 minutes or till the topping is just set, rotating the ring mold a half-turn 3 times. Let stand, uncovered, for 10 minutes. Makes 6 servings.

Saucy Beef and Veal Meatballs

220 calories/serving

A hint of coffee flavor perks up the sauce in this variation of Swedish meatballs.

1 medium onion, chopped (½ cup)
1 tablespoon water
1 slightly beaten egg
2 tablespoons water
½ cup fine dry bread crumbs
½ teaspoon salt
⅛ teaspoon pepper
Dash ground ginger
Dash ground nutmeg
¾ pound lean ground beef
½ pound ground veal
1 cup cold water
1 tablespoon cornstarch
1 teaspoon instant beef bouillon granules
½ teaspoon instant coffee crystals
¼ cup snipped parsley

● In a 2-cup measure micro-cook onion and the 1 tablespoon water, uncovered, on 100% power (HIGH) for 1½ to 2 minutes or till onion is tender; *do not drain.*

● In a mixing bowl stir together beaten egg and the 2 tablespoons water. Stir in onion mixture, fine dry bread crumbs, salt, pepper, ginger, and nutmeg. Add ground beef and veal; mix well. Shape the meat mixture into ½-inch meatballs. In a 12x7½x2-inch baking dish micro-cook meatballs, uncovered, on 100% power (HIGH) for 9 to 11 minutes or till done, re-arranging twice during cooking so least-cooked meatballs are brought to the outside edges of the dish. Drain off fat. Let stand, covered, while preparing sauce.

● For sauce, in a mixing bowl stir together the 1 cup cold water, cornstarch, bouillon granules, and coffee crystals. Micro-cook, uncovered, on 100% power (HIGH) for 3 to 4 minutes or till thickened and bubbly, stirring every minute. Pour sauce over meatballs. Micro-cook, uncovered, on 100% power (HIGH) for 1 to 1½ minutes or till heated through. Sprinkle parsley atop meatballs. Makes 6 servings.

Zucchini Lasagna

279 calories/serving

Zucchini replaces the pasta in this full-flavored entrée.

- 3 medium zucchini, sliced ¼ inch thick (3½ cups)
- ½ pound lean ground beef
- 1 small onion, chopped (¼ cup)
- 1 8-ounce can tomato sauce
- 1 clove garlic, minced
- ½ teaspoon dried basil, crushed
- ¼ teaspoon salt
- ¼ teaspoon dried oregano, crushed
- ⅛ teaspoon pepper
- 1 slightly beaten egg
- ¾ cup low-fat cottage cheese
- 2 tablespoons grated Parmesan cheese
- 1 tablespoon all-purpose flour
- 3 slices mozzarella cheese (4½ ounces total)

● In a 1½-quart casserole micro-cook zucchini and 2 tablespoons *water,* covered, on 100% power (HIGH) for 4 to 6 minutes or till tender, stirring once. Drain in a colander; set aside.

● Crumble ground beef into the 1½-quart casserole; stir in the chopped onion. Micro-cook, uncovered, on 100% power (HIGH) for 3 to 4 minutes or till meat is done and onion is tender, stirring once to break up meat. Drain off fat. Stir in tomato sauce, garlic, basil, salt, oregano, and pepper. Micro-cook, uncovered, on 100% power (HIGH) about 5 minutes or till heated through, stirring once.

● Stir together egg, cottage cheese, and Parmesan cheese. Arrange *half* of the zucchini in a 10x6x2-inch baking dish. Sprinkle with *1½ teaspoons* of the flour. Layer with cottage cheese mixture, then *half* of the meat mixture. Sprinkle with remaining flour. Top with remaining zucchini and remaining meat mixture. Micro-cook, uncovered, on 100% power (HIGH) about 9 minutes or till heated through, rotating the dish a half-turn twice. Top with mozzarella cheese. Micro-cook, uncovered, on 100% power (HIGH) for 1 to 2 minutes or till cheese is melted. Let stand, uncovered, for 5 minutes. Makes 4 servings.

Layering the lasagna casserole

Because the zucchini will water out, add the flour to thicken the released liquid. Sprinkle *1½ teaspoons* of the flour over the first layer of cooked zucchini. Follow with a layer of the cottage cheese mixture, then *half* of the meat mixture. Sprinkle with the remaining flour. Add the remaining zucchini and spread the remaining meat mixture evenly over the top.

Chicken and Dumplings with Vegetables

274 calories/serving

All-American chicken and dumplings evolved from the Chinese dumplings, chu-pao-pa, developed thousands of years ago.

¾ cup frozen peas and carrots
2 tablespoons water
2 tablespoons all-purpose flour
1½ teaspoons instant chicken bouillon granules
½ teaspoon dried basil, crushed
Dash pepper
⅔ cup cold water
⅓ cup skim milk
1 cup coarsely chopped, cooked chicken
½ cup all-purpose flour
1 teaspoon baking powder
1 teaspoon dried parsley flakes
Dash salt
1 slightly beaten egg
1 tablespoon skim milk
1 tablespoon cooking oil
Paprika (optional)

● In a 1½-quart casserole micro-cook the frozen peas and carrots and the 2 tablespoons water, covered, on 100% power (HIGH) for 2 to 3 minutes or till crisp-tender, stirring once. Drain. In a small mixing bowl stir together the 2 tablespoons flour, chicken bouillon granules, basil, and pepper. Stir in the ⅔ cup water and the ⅓ cup skim milk. Stir mixture into vegetables. Micro-cook, uncovered, on 100% power (HIGH) for 3 to 4 minutes or till the mixture is thickened and bubbly, stirring every minute. Stir in the chicken. Let stand, covered, while preparing dumplings.

● For dumplings, in a mixing bowl stir together the ½ cup flour, baking powder, parsley flakes, and salt. Combine the beaten egg, the 1 tablespoon skim milk, and cooking oil; stir into the flour mixture just till moistened. Drop in 6 mounds atop the chicken mixture. Sprinkle with paprika, if desired. Micro-cook, uncovered, on 50% power (MEDIUM) for 4 to 5 minutes or just till dumplings are set. Makes 3 servings.

Micro-Cooking Chicken

Chicken, especially with the skin removed, is ideal for the dieter. And you can save time by taking advantage of the speed of micro-cooking when a recipe, such as Chicken and Dumplings with Vegetables, calls for cooked chicken.

For 1 cup chopped cooked chicken, start with a 1-pound whole *chicken breast*. In a 1½-quart casserole micro-cook the chicken breast and 1 tablespoon *water*, covered, on 100% power (HIGH) for 6 to 7 minutes or till the chicken is done, turning the chicken over and rotating the casserole a half-turn after 4 minutes. Drain and cool the chicken; remove and discard the skin. Remove meat from the bones; chop the meat.

Basil Chicken Saltimbocca

292 calories/serving

Saltimbocca, an Italian word, means "jump in mouth."

3 tablespoons fine dry bread crumbs
2 teaspoons snipped parsley
¼ teaspoon paprika
⅛ teaspoon dried basil, crushed
2 whole large chicken breasts, skinned, halved lengthwise, and boned
2 thin slices fully cooked ham, halved (1½ ounces total)
1 thin slice Swiss cheese, quartered (1½ ounces)
1 small tomato, peeled, seeded, and chopped
Dried basil, crushed
1 teaspoon cooking oil

● Stir together bread crumbs, snipped parsley, paprika, the ⅛ teaspoon basil, and ⅛ teaspoon *salt*; set aside. Place one piece of chicken, boned side up, between two pieces of clear plastic wrap. Working from the center to the edges of the chicken, pound lightly with the flat side of a meat mallet, forming a rectangle about ⅛ inch thick. Remove the clear plastic wrap. Repeat with remaining chicken.
● Place a half slice of ham and a quarter slice of cheese on each chicken breast, trimming if necessary to fit within ¼ inch of the edges. Top with tomato and an additional pinch of basil. Fold in sides of each chicken breast; roll up jelly-roll style. Place seam side down in a shallow baking dish. Brush lightly with cooking oil. Sprinkle with crumb mixture. Micro-cook, uncovered, on 50% power (MEDIUM) for 11 to 13 minutes or till chicken is tender, rotating dish a half-turn every 5 minutes. Garnish with a tomato rose and basil sprigs, if desired. Makes 4 servings.

Calorie-Trimmed Coquilles Saint Jacques

236 calories/serving

Coquilles are the baking shells in which this scallop dish is served. Coquilles may be purchased in kitchen shops.

1 pound fresh *or* frozen scallops
1 cup sliced fresh mushrooms
½ cup dry white wine
3 tablespoons thinly sliced green onion
2 teaspoons lemon juice
1 clove garlic, minced
¼ teaspoon salt
¾ cup skim milk
¼ cup all-purpose flour
¼ teaspoon salt
⅛ teaspoon ground nutmeg
Dash pepper
¼ cup crushed rich round crackers

● Thaw scallops, if frozen.* Halve any large scallops. Rinse and drain the scallops. In a 1½-quart casserole stir together the scallops, mushrooms, wine, onion, lemon juice, garlic, and ¼ teaspoon salt. Micro-cook, covered, on 100% power (HIGH) for 6 to 7 minutes or till the scallops are tender, stirring after 3 minutes. Drain, reserving ¾ cup of the liquid. Set aside while preparing the sauce.
● For sauce, in a 4-cup measure stir together milk, flour, ¼ teaspoon salt, nutmeg, and pepper till smooth. Stir in the reserved ¾ cup liquid. Micro-cook, uncovered, on 100% power (HIGH) for 3 to 4 minutes or till thickened and bubbly, stirring every minute.
● Spoon scallop mixture into 4 individual coquilles, shallow individual casseroles, or 6-ounce custard cups. Pour sauce atop. Sprinkle with crushed crackers. Micro-cook, uncovered, on 100% power (HIGH) for 30 seconds to 1 minute or till heated through. Makes 4 servings.
*Note: To thaw scallops, in a 1½-quart casserole micro-cook frozen scallops, uncovered, on 50% power (MEDIUM) about 7 minutes or till nearly thawed, removing thawed portions twice.

Basil Chicken Saltimbocca

Sweet-and-Sour-Sauced Fish

249 calories/serving

To make a spicier version of this colorful dish, add ⅛ teaspoon crushed red pepper to the sauce.

1   16-ounce package frozen fish fillets
2   medium stalks celery, bias sliced (1 cup)
1   medium green pepper, cut into thin strips (¾ cup)
1   medium carrot, thinly bias sliced (½ cup)
1   tablespoon water
¼   cup packed brown sugar
1   tablespoon cornstarch
1   teaspoon instant chicken bouillon granules
¼   teaspoon garlic powder
¼   teaspoon ground ginger
½   cup cold water
¼   cup red wine vinegar
1   tablespoon soy sauce
3   cups hot cooked rice

● Thaw fish fillets.* Remove skin, if necessary. Cut fish fillets into 1-inch cubes; set aside. In a 10x6x2-inch baking dish combine celery, green pepper, carrot, and the 1 tablespoon water. Cover with clear plastic wrap; vent by leaving a small area unsealed at the edge of the dish. Micro-cook on 100% power (HIGH) for 6 to 8 minutes or till the vegetables are crisp-tender, stirring once.
● Stir the fish cubes into the vegetable mixture. Micro-cook, covered, on 100% power (HIGH) for 3 to 4 minutes or till the fish flakes easily when tested with a fork, stirring once. Drain. Let stand, covered, while preparing sauce.
● For sauce, in a 2-cup measure stir together the brown sugar, cornstarch, bouillon granules, garlic powder, and ginger. Stir in the ½ cup cold water, vinegar, and soy sauce. Micro-cook, uncovered, on 100% power (HIGH) for 2 to 3 minutes or till thickened and bubbly, stirring every minute. Pour sauce over fish mixture; toss to coat fish and vegetables. Serve atop hot cooked rice. Makes 6 servings.
*Note: To thaw fish, in a 10x6x2-inch baking dish micro-cook frozen fish, uncovered, on 50% power (MEDIUM) for 6 to 8 minutes or till just thawed, rotating the dish a half-turn once.

Slimmer Shrimp Newburg

280 calories/serving

Patty shells are puff pastry formed into a cup shape before baking. They go well with this saucy shrimp filling.

1   6-ounce package frozen cooked shrimp
4   frozen patty shells
1¼ cups skim milk
2   tablespoons all-purpose flour
3   beaten egg yolks
2   tablespoons dry white wine
⅛   teaspoon salt
    Paprika
    Fresh parsley sprigs (optional)

● Thaw shrimp.* Drain; set aside. Bake patty shells according to package directions. Meanwhile, in a screw-top jar combine milk and flour. Cover and shake to combine. Pour into a 1-quart casserole. Micro-cook, uncovered, on 100% power (HIGH) for 3 to 4 minutes or till thickened and bubbly, stirring every minute.
● Stir about *half* of the hot mixture into the beaten egg yolks. Return to remaining hot mixture in the casserole. Micro-cook, uncovered, on 50% power (MEDIUM) for 1½ minutes, stirring once. Stir in shrimp, wine, and salt. Micro-cook, uncovered, on 50% power (MEDIUM) about 5 minutes or till heated through, stirring 3 times. Spoon the shrimp mixture into the baked patty shells. Sprinkle with paprika. Garnish with parsley, if desired. Makes 4 servings.
*Note: To thaw shrimp, in a mixing bowl micro-cook shrimp, uncovered, on 50% power (MEDIUM) for 3 to 5 minutes or till nearly thawed, stirring once. Let stand, uncovered, about 6 minutes or till completely thawed.

CHAPTER THREE

SUPER-
FAST
FEASTS

Quickly prepared foods can be calorie-wise treats. These Super-Fast Feasts can be prepared from start to finish in 20 minutes or less. And with that kind of speed, you'll have less time to nibble as you cook, more time for fun and exercise.

Beef-Vegetable Pockets

244 calories/serving

If you quarter this filled-to-the-brim pita, you'll need to eat it with a knife and fork.

½ pound lean ground beef
1½ cups loose-pack frozen
    mixed broccoli, carrots,
    and cauliflower
¼ cup cold water
2 tablespoons soy sauce
2 teaspoons cornstarch
⅛ teaspoon ground ginger
½ of an 8-ounce can sliced
    water chestnuts, drained
3 8-inch pita bread rounds,
    quartered or halved

● Crumble the lean ground beef into a 1-quart casserole. Micro-cook, covered, on 100% power (HIGH) about 3 minutes or till done, stirring twice to break up the ground beef. Drain off fat. Cut up any large pieces in the frozen mixed vegetables. Stir the vegetables into the ground beef. Micro-cook, covered, on 100% power (HIGH) for 3 to 4 minutes or till the vegetables are done, stirring once.

● In a 1-cup measure stir together water, soy sauce, cornstarch, and ginger. Stir soy sauce mixture and water chestnuts into beef-vegetable mixture. Micro-cook, covered, on 100% power (HIGH) for 2 to 3 minutes more or till thickened and bubbly, stirring once. Spoon beef-vegetable mixture into the pita bread quarters or halves. Makes 3 servings.

Beef-Vegetable Soup for Two

149 calories/serving

Members of our taste panel especially liked the character that the basil and thyme added to this wholesome soup.

¼ pound lean ground beef
1 cup loose-pack frozen mixed
    French-cut green beans,
    cauliflower, and carrots
1 cup water
1 8-ounce can tomato sauce
1 teaspoon instant beef
    bouillon granules
¼ teaspoon dried basil,
    crushed
⅛ teaspoon dried thyme,
    crushed
    Dash onion powder
    Dash pepper

● Crumble the lean ground beef into a 1½-quart casserole. Micro-cook, covered, on 100% power (HIGH) for 2 to 3 minutes or till done, stirring once to break up the ground beef. Drain off fat. Stir in vegetables, water, tomato sauce, bouillon granules, basil, thyme, onion powder, and pepper. Micro-cook, covered, on 100% power (HIGH) about 5 minutes or till vegetables are tender and mixture is heated through, stirring once. Ladle into 2 soup bowls. Makes 2 servings.

Beef-Vegetable Pockets

Saucy Cubed Steak

160 calories/serving

One of our food editors suggested serving this main dish with a side dish of cooked, shredded cabbage.

1½ pounds beef cubed steak
1 7½-ounce can semi-
      condensed cream of
      mushroom soup
⅓ cup plain low-fat yogurt
1 tablespoon dry white wine
1 4-ounce can sliced
      mushrooms, drained
   Paprika (optional)

● Place meat in a 12x7½x2-inch baking dish. Cover with clear plastic wrap; vent by leaving a small area unsealed at the edge of the dish. Micro-cook on 100% power (HIGH) for 6 to 8 minutes or till done, turning the meat and rearranging once. Let meat stand, covered, while preparing sauce.

● For sauce, in a 2-cup measure stir together the soup, yogurt, and wine. Stir in mushrooms. Micro-cook, uncovered, on 100% power (HIGH) for 3 to 4 minutes or till heated through, stirring once. Transfer the meat to a serving platter. Pour the sauce atop. Sprinkle with paprika, if desired. Makes 6 servings.

Cooking with Yogurt

For the dieter, low-fat yogurt is a good alternative to sour cream, cream-style cottage cheese, mayonnaise, or salad dressing. A tablespoon of plain low-fat yogurt has only 8 calories compared with 26 calories for sour cream, 15 calories for cream-style cottage cheese, 101 calories for mayonnaise, and 65 calories for salad dressing. Substitute plain low-fat yogurt in many recipes that call for the more calorie-dense products.

Like sour cream, yogurt needs a low cooking temperature and a short heating period to prevent curdling. When using yogurt in a sauce, stir it in at the end of cooking; heat through but *do not boil.* Another tip to prevent curdling is to stabilize the yogurt by stirring in flour or cornstarch.

Finally, you should stir gently when adding yogurt to a mixture. Vigorous stirring causes the yogurt to become thin.

Italian-Style Veal Patties

246 calories/serving

To prevent the Parmesan cheese from becoming soggy, sprinkle it atop the meat patties just before serving.

- 1 beaten egg
- ¼ cup soft bread crumbs (⅓ slice)
- ¼ teaspoon salt
- ¼ teaspoon dried oregano, crushed
- ⅛ teaspoon onion powder
- ⅛ teaspoon dried basil, crushed
- 1 pound ground veal *or* lean ground beef
- ⅓ cup tomato sauce
- ⅛ teaspoon onion powder
- ⅛ teaspoon dried basil, crushed
- 1 tablespoon grated Parmesan cheese

● In a medium mixing bowl stir together the egg, bread crumbs, salt, oregano, ⅛ teaspoon onion powder, and ⅛ teaspoon basil. Add ground veal or beef; mix well. Shape into four ½-inch-thick patties. In an 8x8x2-inch baking dish micro-cook patties, uncovered, on 100% power (HIGH) for 6 to 7 minutes or till done, turning patties and rotating the dish a half-turn once. Let stand, covered, while preparing sauce.

● For sauce, in a 1-cup measure stir together tomato sauce, ⅛ teaspoon onion powder, and ⅛ teaspoon dried basil. Cover with clear plastic wrap; vent by leaving a small area unsealed at the edge of the dish. Micro-cook on 100% power (HIGH) for 1 to 2 minutes or till heated through, stirring once. Transfer meat patties to a serving platter. Pour sauce over patties. Sprinkle some of the Parmesan cheese atop each patty. Makes 4 servings.

Shaping Meat Patties

For even cooking in the microwave oven, uniformity of size and shape is especially important. Turn out uniform burgers by starting with equal portions of meat. Just scoop the meat into a ½-cup measure, then turn out and shape into a patty. Another method is to form ground meat into a roll 4 inches in diameter. You may then cut the roll into ½-inch slices.

Always shape meat patties carefully because too much handling can cause a compact texture.

Fiesta Burgers

Fiesta Burgers

248 calories/serving

To save time, shred the lettuce while the ground beef patties are cooking in the microwave oven.

1 beaten egg
2 teaspoons chili salsa
2 tablespoons toasted wheat germ
1 teaspoon chili powder
½ teaspoon salt
¾ pound lean ground beef
¾ cup chili salsa
2 cups shredded lettuce
2 tablespoons shredded mozzarella cheese
Pickled peppers (optional)

● In a medium mixing bowl stir together egg and the 2 teaspoons salsa. Stir in wheat germ, chili powder, and salt. Add ground beef; mix well. Shape ground beef mixture into four ½-inch-thick patties. In an 8x8x2-inch baking dish micro-cook patties, uncovered, on 100% power (HIGH) for 6 to 7 minutes or till done, turning patties and rotating the dish a half-turn once. Let stand, covered, while preparing sauce.
● For sauce, in a 2-cup measure micro-cook the ¾ cup salsa, uncovered, on 100% power (HIGH) about 2 minutes or till heated through. Divide shredded lettuce among 4 dinner plates. Place beef patties atop lettuce. Pour sauce over patties. Sprinkle each patty with some of the cheese. Garnish with pickled peppers, if desired. Makes 4 servings.

Lamb Chops with Lemon-Mustard Sauce

119 calories/serving

Young lamb meat of high quality should be light to medium pink, with a fine texture and a small amount of muscle.

2 4- to 5-ounce lamb shoulder chops, cut ½ inch thick and trimmed of separable fat
1 teaspoon cooking oil
2 tablespoons water
1½ teaspoons lemon juice
1½ teaspoons Dijon-style mustard
½ teaspoon cornstarch
½ teaspoon instant chicken bouillon granules
⅛ teaspoon garlic powder

● Slash edges of lamb chops to prevent curling. Preheat a 10-inch microwave browning dish on 100% power (HIGH) for 5 minutes. Use a heat-proof pastry brush to brush cooking oil on the bottom of the browning dish. Add the lamb chops. Micro-cook, covered, on 100% power (HIGH) for 2 to 3 minutes or till the lamb chops are done, turning once. Let stand, covered, while preparing sauce.
● For sauce, in a 1-cup measure stir together the water, lemon juice, Dijon-style mustard, cornstarch, chicken bouillon granules, and garlic powder. Micro-cook, covered, on 100% power (HIGH) for 1 to 2 minutes or till thickened and bubbly, stirring every 30 seconds. Transfer the lamb chops to 2 individual dinner plates. Spoon sauce over the lamb chops. Makes 2 servings.

Sweet-and-Sour Ham

145 calories/serving

For a complete meal, serve this recipe with Parslied Rice. The rice adds only 89 calories per serving.

½ pound fully cooked ham, trimmed of separable fat
1 11-ounce can pineapple tidbits and mandarin orange sections, drained
½ of an 8-ounce can sliced water chestnuts, drained
2 tablespoons brown sugar
2 teaspoons cornstarch
3 tablespoons water
2 tablespoons red wine vinegar
1 teaspoon soy sauce
Dash ground ginger
Parslied Rice (optional)

● Cut ham into bite-size strips. In a 1½-quart casserole stir together ham, pineapple tidbits and mandarin orange sections, and water chestnuts. Micro-cook, covered, on 100% power (HIGH) for 2½ to 3½ minutes or till heated through, stirring once. Let stand, covered, while preparing sauce.
● For sauce, in a 2-cup measure stir together the brown sugar and cornstarch. Stir in the water, vinegar, soy sauce, and ground ginger. Micro-cook, uncovered, on 100% power (HIGH) for 1½ to 2 minutes or till the sauce is thickened and bubbly, stirring every minute.
● Toss together the sauce and the ham mixture. Serve over Parslied Rice, if desired. Makes 3 servings.

Parslied Rice: In a 1-quart cassserole stir together ¾ cup warm *water* and 1 tablespoon dried *parsley flakes*. Micro-cook, covered, on 100% power (HIGH) for 2 to 3 minutes or till mixture is boiling. Stir in ¾ cup quick-cooking *rice*. Let stand, covered, at least 5 minutes.

Ham and Kraut

210 calories/serving

To balance the sour flavor with the other ingredients, rinse the sauerkraut with cold water before you drain it.

½ cup apple juice *or* apple cider
2 tablespoons brown sugar
1 teaspoon cornstarch
1 small apple, cored and chopped (about ⅔ cup)
½ of a small onion, chopped (¼ cup)
1 tablespoon water
1 pound fully cooked ham, trimmed of separable fat and cut into bite-size strips
1 16-ounce can sauerkraut, rinsed and drained

● In a 2-cup measure stir together apple juice or apple cider, brown sugar, and cornstarch. Micro-cook, uncovered, on 100% power (HIGH) for 1½ to 2 minutes or till thickened and bubbly, stirring every minute.
● In a 2-quart casserole combine chopped apple, chopped onion, and water. Micro-cook, covered, on 100% power (HIGH) for 1 to 2 minutes or just till apple and onion are tender. Stir in ham, sauerkraut, and apple juice mixture. Micro-cook, covered, on 100% power (HIGH) for 5 to 6 minutes or till mixture is heated through, stirring every 3 minutes. Makes 6 servings.

Chicken Ramekins

256 calories/serving

Since not all yogurt is low-fat, you'll need to check the label carefully when looking for this product.

½ teaspoon shortening
1 beaten egg
3 tablespoons plain low-fat yogurt
3 tablespoons fine dry bread crumbs
1 teaspoon dried parsley flakes
¼ teaspoon dried marjoram *or* dried basil, crushed
⅛ teaspoon salt
⅛ teaspoon onion powder
1 5-ounce can chunk-style chicken, cut up
2 tablespoons plain low-fat yogurt
   Paprika (optional)

● Lightly grease two 6-ounce custard cups with shortening; set aside. In a mixing bowl stir together the egg and the 3 tablespoons yogurt. Stir in the bread crumbs, parsley, marjoram or basil, salt, and onion powder.

● Stir *undrained* chicken into egg mixture. Spoon into prepared custard cups. Cover each cup loosely with waxed paper. Micro-cook on 100% power (HIGH) for 3 minutes or till almost firm. Let stand, covered, for 2 minutes.

● With a narrow metal spatula loosen edges; unmold onto a serving plate. Dollop each with some of the 2 tablespoons yogurt. Sprinkle with paprika, if desired. Makes 2 servings.

Tarragon Chicken

219 calories/serving

To speed the preparation of this recipe even more, purchase the chicken breasts that already are boned and skinned.

½ cup cold water
¼ cup dry white wine
1 tablespoon cornstarch
1 tablespoon lemon juice
2 teaspoons instant chicken bouillon granules
1 teaspoon dried tarragon, crushed
2 whole large chicken breasts, skinned, halved lengthwise, and boned
   Fresh tarragon sprigs (optional)
   Orange wedges (optional)

● For sauce, in a 10x6x2-inch baking dish stir together cold water, white wine, cornstarch, lemon juice, bouillon granules, and the dried tarragon. Micro-cook, uncovered, on 100% power (HIGH) for 3 to 4 minutes or till thickened and bubbly, stirring every minute.

● Arrange chicken breasts atop sauce in baking dish; turn to coat with sauce. Cover with clear plastic wrap; vent by leaving a small area unsealed at the edge of the dish. Micro-cook on 100% power (HIGH) for 5 to 7 minutes or till tender, rearranging and turning chicken breasts once.

● Transfer chicken breasts to a serving platter. Spoon the sauce over the chicken. Garnish with fresh tarragon sprigs and orange wedges, if desired. Makes 4 servings.

Turkey and Carrot Patties

272 calories/serving

Try ground turkey as an alternative to ground beef. It's lower in calories and fat than most other ground meats.

1 small carrot, shredded
   (¼ cup)
2 tablespoons water
½ teaspoon minced dried
   onion
1 beaten egg
2 tablespoons fine dry bread
   crumbs
¼ teaspoon salt
¼ teaspoon poultry seasoning
½ pound ground raw turkey

● In a mixing bowl stir together shredded carrot, water, and minced dried onion. Cover with clear plastic wrap; vent by leaving a small area unsealed at the edge of the bowl. Micro-cook on 100% power (HIGH) about 1½ minutes or till the shredded carrot is tender. Drain.

● Stir beaten egg, fine dry bread crumbs, salt, and poultry seasoning into the carrot mixture. Add ground raw turkey; mix well. Shape the meat mixture into two ½-inch-thick patties; mixture will be soft.

● Place patties in a shallow baking dish. Cover with clear plastic wrap; vent by leaving a small area unsealed at the edge of the dish. Micro-cook on 100% power (HIGH) for 4 to 5 minutes or till nearly done, rotating the dish a half-turn every 2 minutes. Let stand, covered, for 1 minute. Makes 2 servings.

Salmon Patties

325 calories/serving

Shredded cucumber adds a pleasing freshness and crunch to these salmon patties.

1 beaten egg
½ cup soft bread crumbs
   (½ slice)
½ of a small cucumber,
   shredded (⅓ cup)
½ teaspoon dried dillweed
   Dash pepper
1 7¾-ounce can salmon,
   drained, flaked, and skin
   and bones removed
1 teaspoon cooking oil
2 tablespoons plain low-fat
   yogurt
¼ teaspoon dried dillweed
½ of a small cucumber, very
   thinly sliced (optional)
   Fresh dillweed (optional)
   Lemon wedges (optional)

● In a mixing bowl stir together egg, bread crumbs, shredded cucumber, the ½ teaspoon dillweed, and pepper. Add salmon; mix well. Shape into two ½-inch-thick patties.

● Preheat a 10-inch microwave browning dish on 100% power (HIGH) for 5 minutes. Use a heat-proof pastry brush to brush cooking oil on the bottom of the dish. Place the salmon patties in the browning dish. Micro-cook, uncovered, on 100% power (HIGH) for 4 to 5 minutes or till heated through, turning patties over once.

● Meanwhile, in a small bowl stir together yogurt and the ¼ teaspoon dillweed. Arrange cucumber slices on 2 plates, if desired. Top with salmon patties. Dollop yogurt mixture atop patties. If desired, garnish with fresh dillweed and serve with lemon wedges. Makes 2 servings.

Salmon Patties

1 Testing the doneness of fish

Micro-cook the fish for the minimum amount of time indicated in the recipe. Insert the tines of a table fork into the fish at a 45-degree angle and twist the fork gently.

If the fish flakes and is opaque, it is done perfectly. If it resists flaking and still has a translucent quality, it is not done and should be micro-cooked a little longer.

2 Draining the Halibut Mandarin

Before you spoon the sauce over the fish, drain well to keep the fish from watering out and making the sauce too thin. Use a slotted spoon to transfer the fish portion from the baking dish to a paper towel. Immediately move the fish portion to a dinner plate and top it with the sauce.

Halibut Mandarin

173 calories/serving

For this recipe, be sure to purchase the individually frozen fish portions that aren't breaded.

1 11½-ounce package frozen halibut *or* other fish portions
2 tablespoons water
2 teaspoons cornstarch
1 teaspoon dried parsley flakes
½ teaspoon instant chicken bouillon granules
½ cup orange juice
1 tablespoon dry white wine
1 teaspoon diet margarine
1 11-ounce can mandarin orange sections, drained

● Place fish portions in a shallow baking dish. Sprinkle with water. Cover with clear plastic wrap; vent by leaving a small area unsealed at the edge of the dish. Micro-cook on 100% power (HIGH) for 6 to 9 minutes or till fish flakes easily when tested with a fork. Let stand, covered, while preparing sauce.

● For sauce, in a small bowl stir together cornstarch, parsley flakes, and bouillon granules. Stir in orange juice and wine. Micro-cook, uncovered, on 100% power (HIGH) for 2 to 3 minutes or till thickened and bubbly, stirring every minute. Stir in the diet margarine. Gently stir in the mandarin orange sections. Drain the fish well; place on 4 dinner plates. Spoon the sauce over the fish. Makes 4 servings.

Buying and Storing Frozen Fish

If a retailer is careless, frozen fish may thaw and refreeze repeatedly, causing loss of flavor and risk of spoilage before purchase. Avoid purchasing damaged fish by watching for these signs of thawing and refreezing:
● Packages that are no longer their original shape.
● Packages with torn wrappers.
● Packages with frost or blood visible anywhere.
   Once you've purchased the fish, be sure that it stays frozen until you can place it in your freezer.

Depending on the type of fish, it will retain its quality when kept at 0° or lower for two to six months. You can store cod, haddock, ocean perch, pike, or other lean species of fish about six months. Species containing a large proportion of fat to lean, such as salmon, mackerel, or lake trout, should not be frozen longer than two months.
   The best way to thaw fish is in the refrigerator in the original wrapping. A 1-pound package of frozen fish will take about 24 hours to thaw.

Italian-Style Fish

185 calories/serving

Freeze the unused tomatoes and peppers. To thaw later, micro-cook on 30% power (MEDIUM-LOW) about 3 minutes.

1   11½-ounce package frozen
    fish portions
2   tablespoons water
½   of a 10-ounce can tomatoes
    and green chili peppers,
    cut up
1   2½-ounce jar sliced
    mushrooms, drained
1   teaspoon cornstarch
½   teaspoon sugar
¼   teaspoon dried basil,
    crushed
2   tablespoons shredded
    mozzarella cheese

● Place frozen fish portions in a shallow baking dish. Sprinkle with water. Cover with clear plastic wrap; vent by leaving a small area unsealed at the edge of the baking dish. Micro-cook on 100% power (HIGH) for 6 to 9 minutes or till fish flakes easily when tested with a fork. Let fish stand, covered, while preparing the sauce.

● For sauce, in a 2-cup measure stir together *undrained* tomatoes and green chili peppers, sliced mushrooms, cornstarch, sugar, and dried basil. Micro-cook, uncovered, on 100% power (HIGH) for 2 to 3 minutes or till thickened and bubbly, stirring every minute.

● Drain fish well. Transfer to a nonmetal serving platter. Pour the sauce over fish. Sprinkle with cheese. Micro-cook, uncovered, on 100% power (HIGH) for 30 seconds to 1 minute or till cheese is melted. Makes 4 servings.

Hot Shrimp Salad

205 calories/serving

You can serve the sweet-and-sour salad dressing with other savory salads, too. (Pictured on the front cover.)

1   16-ounce can orange and
    grapefruit sections
4   cups torn leaf lettuce
1   small onion, thinly sliced
    and separated into rings
    Pepper
2   tablespoons brown sugar
1½ teaspoons cornstarch
⅛   teaspoon ground ginger
    Dash garlic powder
4   teaspoons wine vinegar
1½ teaspoons soy sauce
2   6-ounce packages frozen
    cooked shrimp
1   cup frozen crinkle-cut
    carrots

● Drain orange and grapefruit sections, reserving ⅓ *cup* of the juice. Set juice aside. In a large salad bowl toss together torn lettuce, onion rings, and orange and grapefruit sections. Sprinkle generously with pepper.

● For salad dressing, in a 2-cup measure stir together brown sugar, cornstarch, ginger, and garlic powder. Stir in wine vinegar, soy sauce, and the reserved juice. Micro-cook, uncovered, on 100% power (HIGH) for 2 to 3 minutes or till thickened and bubbly, stirring every minute. Let stand, covered, while preparing shrimp and carrots.

● In a 1½-quart casserole combine shrimp and carrots. Micro-cook, covered, on 100% power (HIGH) for 5 to 7 minutes or till shrimp are heated through and carrots are tender, stirring twice. Drain. Place shrimp and carrots atop lettuce mixture. Pour hot salad dressing atop. Toss well. Makes 4 servings.

CHAPTER FOUR

ALREADY
◆
READY

If you
have trouble fitting
dieting into your life-
style, this chapter is
for you. Each of the main
dishes is designed so you
can cook it right away
or make it ahead, freeze,
and then cook it another
time. Because micro-
wave timings are given
for single servings, these
recipes are especially
useful if you're
dieting alone.

Stuffed Steak Roll and Noodles

376 calories/serving

Tapioca is used as the thickener in the sauce, because it will freeze and reheat without breaking down.

2⅔ ounces medium noodles
¾ pound beef top round steak, cut ½ inch thick and trimmed of separable fat
1 beaten egg
2 medium carrots, shredded (1 cup)
¼ cup fine dry bread crumbs
2 tablespoons sliced green onion
¼ teaspoon salt
¼ teaspoon dried thyme, crushed
1 13¾-ounce can beef broth
¼ cup dry red wine
2 tablespoons quick-cooking tapioca
Dash pepper
Fresh parsley sprigs (optional)

● Cook noodles according to package directions. Drain; cover and set aside. Meanwhile, use a meat mallet to pound steak to ¼-inch thickness. In a bowl stir together egg, carrot, bread crumbs, green onion, salt, and thyme.

● Spread the carrot mixture over the round steak. Roll up jelly-roll style, beginning with a short side. Tie with string. Place, seam side up, on a nonmetal rack in a shallow baking dish. Micro-cook, uncovered, on 50% power (MEDIUM) for 5 minutes. Turn over the meat roll. Micro-cook, uncovered, on 50% power (MEDIUM) for 6 to 8 minutes more or till the meat is done, rotating the dish a half-turn every 2 minutes. Let stand, covered, while preparing sauce.

● For sauce, in a 4-cup measure stir together beef broth, wine, tapioca, and pepper. Let stand 5 minutes. Micro-cook, uncovered, on 100% power (HIGH) for 3 to 4 minutes or till boiling, stirring every minute. Micro-cook, uncovered, on 50% power (MEDIUM) for 5 minutes more, stirring twice.

● Remove string from meat roll. Cut into 12 slices. Spoon noodles into 4 individual casseroles. Place 3 meat slices atop noodles in each casserole. Pour sauce over all. Prepare according to directions below. Makes 4 single-serving entrées.

For immediate serving: Cover 1 individual casserole with clear plastic wrap; vent by leaving a small area unsealed at the edge of the dish. Micro-cook on 100% power (HIGH) for 1 to 2 minutes or till heated through, rotating dish a half-turn once. Garnish with fresh parsley sprig, if desired. If additional servings are desired, cover and repeat micro-cooking.

For later serving: Cover all casseroles to be frozen with moisture- and vaporproof wrap. Seal, label, and freeze for up to 2 months. Remove moisture- and vaporproof wrap from 1 individual casserole. Cover with clear plastic wrap; vent by leaving a small area unsealed at the edge of the casserole. Micro-cook on 70% power (MEDIUM-HIGH) for 6 to 8 minutes or till heated through, rotating the casserole a half-turn once. Garnish the casserole with a fresh parsley sprig, if desired. If additional servings are desired, remove moisture- and vaporproof wrap and repeat micro-cooking.

Stuffed Steak Roll and Noodles

Stuffed Peppers

263 calories/serving

Don't discard the tops of the green peppers; chop them and add to your next tossed salad.

4 large green peppers
  Salt
¾ pound lean ground beef
1 medium onion, chopped
    (½ cup)
1 8-ounce can tomato sauce
1½ teaspoons cornstarch
1 8¾-ounce can whole kernel
    corn, drained
1 teaspoon chili powder
¼ teaspoon salt
¼ teaspoon ground cumin
2 teaspoons fine dry bread
    crumbs

● Use a knife to cut the tops from green peppers. Discard seeds and membranes. Place peppers, cut side up, in an 8x8x2-inch baking dish. Cover the peppers with clear plastic wrap; vent by leaving a small area unsealed at the edge of the dish. Micro-cook on 100% power (HIGH) for 3 minutes. Remove peppers; drain off any liquid in the baking dish. Lightly sprinkle the insides of peppers with salt. Set aside.

● In the 8x8x2-inch baking dish micro-cook ground beef and chopped onion, uncovered, on 100% power (HIGH) for 4 to 5 minutes or till the meat is brown, stirring twice to break up meat. Drain off fat.

● Stir together tomato sauce and cornstarch. Stir tomato sauce mixture, corn, chili powder, salt, and cumin into ground beef mixture. Micro-cook, uncovered, on 100% power (HIGH) for 2 to 3 minutes or till thickened and bubbly, stirring every minute. Place each green pepper in an individual casserole. Spoon meat mixture into peppers. Sprinkle *each* with *½ teaspoon* of the bread crumbs. Prepare according to directions below. Makes 4 single-serving entrées.

For immediate serving: Cover 1 individual casserole with clear plastic wrap; vent by leaving a small area unsealed at the edge of the casserole. Micro-cook on 50% power (MEDIUM) for 5 to 7 minutes or till the ground meat mixture is heated through and the green pepper is nearly tender, rotating the dish a half-turn once. Let stand, covered, for 3 minutes. If additional servings are desired, cover and repeat micro-cooking.

For later serving: Cover all casseroles to be frozen with moisture- and vaporproof wrap. Seal, label, and freeze for up to 2 months. Remove moisture- and vaporproof wrap from 1 individual casserole. Cover with clear plastic wrap; vent by leaving a small area unsealed at the edge of the casserole. Micro-cook on 70% power (MEDIUM-HIGH) for 4 minutes. Remove the clear plastic wrap. Micro-cook, uncovered, on 50% power (MEDIUM) for 5 to 7 minutes or till the meat mixture is heated through and the pepper is nearly tender, rotating the dish a half-turn once. Let stand, covered, for 3 minutes. If additional servings are desired, remove moisture- and vaporproof wrap and repeat micro-cooking.

1 Preparing the green peppers

Cut about ½ inch off the top of each green pepper. Pull the seeds and membranes out of the insides of the peppers and discard them.

2 Covering the baking dish

When covering the baking dish before precooking the peppers, remember to leave an area at the edge of the dish unsealed. This allows the steam to escape.

3 Filling the green peppers

Evenly divide the meat mixture into fourths before you fill the green peppers. This will assure that each serving is an equal amount.

After you've filled each green pepper, sprinkle the tops of each with some of the bread crumbs. Then micro-cook or freeze as directed in the recipe.

Stuffed Cabbage Rolls

193 calories/serving

You can use 16 small cabbage leaves instead of 8 large ones.

1 8-ounce can tomato sauce
1 small carrot, shredded
    (¼ cup)
2 tablespoons water
¼ teaspoon dried basil,
    crushed
¼ teaspoon dried oregano,
    crushed
8 large cabbage leaves
1 beaten egg
⅓ cup fine dry seasoned bread
    crumbs
2 stalks celery, finely chopped
1 small onion, finely chopped
    (¼ cup)
¼ teaspoon salt
    Dash garlic powder
    Dash pepper
1 pound ground raw turkey
¼ cup water

● For sauce, combine first 5 ingredients. Micro-cook, covered, on 100% power (HIGH) for 2 minutes. Set aside. Remove center veins from cabbage leaves. Micro-cook cabbage, covered, on 100% power (HIGH) for 3 to 5 minutes or till limp.

● Combine egg, crumbs, celery, onion, salt, garlic powder, and pepper. Add turkey; mix well. Place on cabbage. Fold in sides; roll up. Place 2 rolls in each of 4 individual casseroles. Sprinkle each casserole with some of the ¼ cup water. Micro-cook all 4 casseroles, covered, on 100% power (HIGH) about 11 minutes or till done, rearranging once. Drain; top with sauce. Prepare according to directions below. Makes 4 single-serving entrées.

For immediate serving: Micro-cook 1 casserole, covered, on 100% power (HIGH) for 2 to 3 minutes or till sauce is heated through. Repeat for additional servings.

For later serving: Cover casseroles with moisture- and vapor-proof wrap. Seal, label, and freeze. Remove wrap from 1 casserole. Micro-cook, covered, on 70% power (MEDIUM-HIGH) for 5 to 7 minutes or till hot. Repeat for additional servings.

1 Micro-cooking cabbage leaves

To remove the center vein of each cabbage leaf, use a sharp paring knife to cut along both sides of the vein, keeping the leaf in one piece. Layer the leaves in a shallow baking dish.

Cover with clear plastic wrap; vent by leaving a small area unsealed at the edge of the baking dish. Micro-cook the cabbage leaves on 100% power (HIGH) for 3 to 5 minutes or till they are limp and will fold easily.

2 Forming the cabbage rolls

Divide the ground turkey mixture into eight equal portions. Place one portion on each cabbage leaf. (If you are using 16 small cabbage leaves instead of the 8 large leaves, overlap 2 leaves for each portion of ground turkey mixture.) Fold in the sides of each leaf and roll up, starting at one unfolded end.

3 Serving the cabbage rolls

After micro-cooking the cabbage rolls, drain off any excess liquid. Spoon the sauce atop the rolls in each individual casserole. Then either micro-cook the cabbage rolls for immediate serving or wrap the casseroles in moisture- and vaporproof wrap and freeze for serving later.

Elegant Chicken and Grapes

252 calories/serving

You can use either green or red grapes in the sauce.

2 whole large chicken breasts, skinned and halved lengthwise
2 tablespoons water
½ cup apricot nectar
2 tablespoons dry white wine
1½ teaspoons quick-cooking tapioca
¼ teaspoon dried rosemary, crushed
1 cup halved and seeded grapes
   Parsley sprigs (optional)

● Place chicken in an 8x8x2-inch baking dish. Sprinkle with water. Cover with clear plastic wrap; vent by leaving a small area unsealed at the edge of the dish. Micro-cook on 100% power (HIGH) for 5 to 7 minutes or till tender, rotating the dish a quarter-turn twice.

● Meanwhile, for sauce, in a 2-cup measure stir together the apricot nectar, wine, tapioca, and rosemary. Let stand for 5 minutes. Micro-cook, uncovered, on 100% power (HIGH) for 1 to 2 minutes or till boiling. Micro-cook, uncovered, on 50% power (MEDIUM) for 3 minutes more, stirring twice.

● Place a chicken breast half in each of 4 individual casseroles. Spoon some of the grapes atop each casserole. Pour sauce atop grapes and chicken. Prepare according to directions below. Makes 4 single-serving entrées.

For immediate serving: Cover 1 individual casserole with clear plastic wrap; vent by leaving a small area unsealed at the edge of the casserole. Micro-cook on 100% power (HIGH) for 1 to 2 minutes or till the sauce and chicken are heated through. Garnish with a parsley sprig, if desired. If additional servings are desired, cover and repeat micro-cooking.

For later serving: Cover all casseroles to be frozen with moisture- and vaporproof wrap. Seal, label, and freeze for up to 2 months. Remove moisture- and vaporproof wrap from 1 individual casserole. Cover with clear plastic wrap; vent by leaving a small area unsealed at the edge of the casserole. Micro-cook on 70% power (MEDIUM-HIGH) for 5 to 7 minutes or till heated through, rotating the casserole a half-turn once. Garnish with a parsley sprig, if desired. If additional servings are desired, remove moisture- and vaporproof wrap and repeat micro-cooking.

Elegant Chicken
and Grapes

Stuffed Chicken Breasts

284 calories/serving

Spanish explorers discovered allspice in the West Indies. The spice tastes like a blend of cloves, cinnamon, and nutmeg.

2 whole large chicken breasts, skinned, halved lengthwise, and boned
¾ cup water
¼ cup long grain rice
1 small carrot, shredded (¼ cup)
2 tablespoons snipped parsley
1 tablespoon sliced green onion
1 teaspoon instant chicken bouillon granules
Dash pepper
1¼ cups orange juice
2 teaspoons quick-cooking tapioca
⅛ teaspoon ground allspice

● Place 1 piece of chicken, boned side up, between two pieces of clear plastic wrap. Working from center to edges, pound lightly with the smooth side of a meat mallet, forming a rectangle about ⅛ inch thick. Remove plastic wrap. Repeat with remaining chicken pieces.

● In a 1-quart casserole stir together water, rice, carrot, parsley, green onion, bouillon granules, and pepper. Micro-cook, covered, on 100% power (HIGH) for 5 minutes. Micro-cook, covered, on 50% power (MEDIUM) for 7 to 9 minutes or till all of the liquid is absorbed.

● Spoon some of the rice mixture atop each chicken piece. Fold in sides; roll up jelly-roll style. Place each filled chicken breast, seam side down, in an individual casserole.

● For sauce, in a 2-cup measure stir together orange juice, tapioca, and allspice. Let stand for 5 minutes. Micro-cook, uncovered, on 100% power (HIGH) for 3 to 4 minutes or till boiling, stirring every minute. Micro-cook, uncovered, on 50% power (MEDIUM) for 5 minutes more, stirring twice. Pour some sauce atop each filled chicken breast. Prepare according to directions below. Makes 4 single-serving entrées.

For immediate serving: Cover 1 individual casserole with clear plastic wrap; vent by leaving a small area unsealed at the edge of the casserole. Micro-cook on 50% power (MEDIUM) for 8 to 10 minutes or till chicken is tender, rotating the casserole a half-turn after 5 minutes. If additional servings are desired, cover and repeat micro-cooking.

For later serving: Cover all casseroles to be frozen with moisture- and vaporproof wrap. Seal, label, and freeze for up to 2 months. Remove moisture- and vaporproof wrap from 1 individual casserole. Cover with clear plastic wrap; vent by leaving a small area unsealed at the edge of the casserole. Micro-cook on 70% power (MEDIUM-HIGH) for 6 minutes, rotating the casserole a half-turn once. Micro-cook on 50% power (MEDIUM) for 4 to 6 minutes or till chicken is tender, rotating the casserole a half-turn twice. If additional servings are desired, remove moisture- and vaporproof wrap and repeat micro-cooking.

Wrapping Main-Dish Casseroles for Freezing

When you choose to freeze the individual casseroles from this chapter, be sure to properly wrap the foods to get the best results. The recipes say to use moisture- and vaporproof wrap—that means heavy foil, heavy plastic bags, or freezer paper. Or, if your casseroles have lids that fit them, you can cover the casserole with the lid and fix it in place by wrapping freezer tape around the edges to make a leakproof seal.

Two-Cheese Turkey Bake

331 calories/serving

Two cheeses contribute to the richness of this one-dish meal.

5 lasagna noodles
1 small onion, chopped (¼ cup)
½ of a small green pepper, chopped (¼ cup)
2 tablespoons water
1 cup chopped cooked turkey *or* chicken
1 7½-ounce can semi-condensed cream of mushroom soup
¼ cup chopped pimiento
¾ teaspoon dried basil, crushed
¾ cup low-fat cottage cheese
¾ cup shredded American cheese (3 ounces)

● Cook noodles according to package directions; drain. Cover; set aside. Combine onion, green pepper, and water. Cover with clear plastic wrap; vent by leaving a small area unsealed at the edge of the dish. Micro-cook on 100% power (HIGH) about 2 minutes or till tender. Drain.

● Stir together turkey or chicken, soup, pimiento, basil, and onion mixture. In 4 individual au gratin dishes place *half* of the noodles, cutting to fit. Top with *half* of the turkey mixture, *half* of the cottage cheese, and *half* of the American cheese. Repeat the layers in each au gratin dish. Prepare according to directions below. Makes 4 single-serving entrées.

For immediate serving: Cover 1 individual au gratin dish with clear plastic wrap; vent by leaving a small area unsealed at the edge of the dish. Micro-cook on 100% power (HIGH) for 4 to 5 minutes or till heated through, rotating the dish a quarter-turn every 2 minutes. If additional servings are desired, cover and repeat micro-cooking.

For later serving: Cover all au gratin dishes to be frozen with moisture- and vaporproof wrap. Seal, label, and freeze for up to 2 months. Remove moisture- and vaporproof wrap from 1 individual au gratin dish. Cover with clear plastic wrap; vent by leaving a small area unsealed at the edge of the dish. Micro-cook on 70% power (MEDIUM-HIGH) for 6 to 8 minutes or till heated through, rotating the dish a quarter-turn every 2 minutes. If additional servings are desired, remove the moisture- and vaporproof wrap and repeat micro-cooking.

Curried Shrimp and Rice

238 calories/serving

This recipe gives a range on the amount of curry powder, so you can vary it to suit your taste.

½ cup long grain rice
1 10¾-ounce can condensed
     cream of celery soup
¼ cup sliced green onion
¼ cup dry white wine
1 to 2 teaspoons curry powder
2 6-ounce packages frozen
     cooked shrimp
½ of a small zucchini,
     shredded (½ cup)

● Cook the rice according to package directions. Cover and set aside. In a 1½-quart casserole stir together the cream of celery soup, the sliced green onion, the dry white wine, and the curry powder. Micro-cook, covered, on 50% power (MEDIUM) for 5 to 7 minutes or till heated through. In a colander run cold water over the shrimp just till they can be broken apart; drain well. Stir shrimp into soup mixture.

● Stir the shredded zucchini into the cooked rice. Spoon rice mixture into 4 individual casseroles. Spoon soup mixture atop. Prepare according to the directions below. Makes 4 single-serving entrées.

For immediate serving: Cover 1 individual casserole with clear plastic wrap; vent by leaving a small area unsealed at the edge of the casserole. Micro-cook on 100% power (HIGH) for 2 to 3 minutes or till the shrimp and rice are heated through, rotating the casserole a half-turn once. If additional servings are desired, cover and repeat micro-cooking.

For later serving: Cover all casseroles to be frozen with moisture- and vaporproof wrap. Seal, label, and freeze for up to 2 months. Remove moisture- and vaporproof wrap from 1 individual casserole. Cover with clear plastic wrap; vent by leaving a small area unsealed at the edge of the casserole. Micro-cook on 70% power (MEDIUM-HIGH) for 8 to 10 minutes or till heated through, rotating the casserole a half-turn every 3 minutes. If additional servings are desired, remove moisture- and vaporproof wrap and repeat micro-cooking.

CHAPTER FIVE

MEALS
◆
ON THE
◆
GO

When
away-from-home meal
options are in conflict
with your goals as a dieter,
try a take-along meal.
This chapter features recipes you can prepare in
your microwave oven at
home and take with you
to work, school, or wher-
ever. And if you have
access to a microwave
oven at mealtime, we also
included some recipes
which you can cook just
before you are ready
to eat.

Savory Soup

259 calories/serving

Using ground beef in this basil-seasoned soup means the cooking time is short.

1 small carrot, thinly sliced
     (¼ cup)
1 tablespoon chopped onion
1 tablespoon water
¼ pound lean ground beef
½ cup tomato sauce
¼ cup water
¼ teaspoon sugar
¼ teaspoon dried basil,
     crushed
   Dash salt
   Dash garlic powder

● Up to 6 hours before mealtime, in a 4-cup measure stir together carrot, onion, and the 1 tablespoon water. Cover with clear plastic wrap; vent by leaving a small area unsealed at the edge of the 4-cup measure. Micro-cook on 100% power (HIGH) for 1½ minutes.

● Crumble ground beef into the 4-cup measure. Stir beef into partially cooked vegetables. Micro-cook, uncovered, on 100% power (HIGH) for 1½ minutes, stirring once to break up. Drain off liquid.

● Stir in tomato sauce, the ¼ cup water, sugar, basil, salt, and garlic powder. Micro-cook, uncovered, on 100% power (HIGH) for 3½ to 4 minutes or till boiling. Pour soup into a small vacuum bottle; seal. Pack soup and a spoon to take along. Makes 1 serving.

Open-Face Chili Sandwich

286 calories/serving

Make Savory Soup one day and use the leftover ground beef and tomato sauce to make this spicy sandwich the next day.

¼ pound lean ground beef
2 tablespoons chopped onion
2 tablespoons chopped celery
¼ cup tomato sauce
½ teaspoon cornstarch
¼ to ½ teaspoon chili powder
   Dash garlic powder
1 slice whole wheat bread

● Crumble ground beef into a 20-ounce casserole. Stir in onion and celery. Micro-cook, uncovered, on 100% power (HIGH) for 2 to 3 minutes or till the meat is done and the vegetables are tender, stirring once. Drain off liquid.

● Stir in tomato sauce, cornstarch, chili powder, and garlic powder. Micro-cook, covered, on 100% power (HIGH) for 1 to 2 minutes or till slightly thickened and bubbly, stirring every 30 seconds. Cool. Cover and refrigerate for 2 to 24 hours.

● Up to 6 hours before mealtime, pack chilled mixture in an air-tight, microwave-safe container. Place bread in a clear plastic bag; seal. Pack meat mixture, bread, a microwave-safe paper plate or a nonmetal plate, and a fork to take along in an insulated lunch box with an ice pack.

● At mealtime, micro-cook meat mixture on 100% power (HIGH) for 1½ to 2 minutes or till heated through. Place bread on plate. Top with meat mixture. Makes 1 serving.

Savory Soup

1 Preparing the potato for the topping mixture

Before packing to take along, scrub the potato thoroughly and remove any sprouts and green areas. Prick the skin.

At mealtime micro-cook the unwrapped potato, uncovered, on 100% power (HIGH) for 3 to 5 minutes or till potato is nearly fork-tender, rotating once. Let stand, uncovered, for 5 minutes to finish cooking. When potato is done, roll gently under your hand to loosen pulp. (Use a paper towel to protect your hand from heat.) With the knife, make a lengthwise slit in the top of the potato. Press the ends and push up, as shown.

2 Topping the cooked potato

As soon as you spoon the hot chicken-salsa mixture into the cooked potato, you're ready to enjoy a satisfying, take-along meal.

Although the preparation steps are simple, you will need to pack a full set of utensils for putting this recipe together.

Beef and Tomato Sandwich

266 calories/serving

Micro-cooking this sandwich on a paper towel prevents the bottom slice of bread from becoming soggy.

½ of a 3-ounce package thinly sliced smoked beef, torn into bite-size pieces
½ of a small tomato, seeded and chopped (¼ cup)
2 tablespoons shredded cheddar cheese
2 slices whole wheat bread, halved, *or* ½ of an 8-inch pita bread round
¼ cup coarsely shredded lettuce

● Up to 6 hours before mealtime, in a clear plastic bag combine beef, tomato, and cheese; seal. In 2 separate clear plastic bags place the bread slices or pita half and the lettuce; seal. Pack meat mixture, bread, lettuce, and a paper towel to take along in an insulated lunch box with an ice pack.

● At mealtime, if using whole wheat bread, place 2 bread halves on the paper towel. Place the meat mixture atop the bread. Or, if using the pita half, place meat mixture in pita half and place on the paper towel. Micro-cook, uncovered, on 100% power (HIGH) for 30 seconds to 1 minute or till meat mixture is heated through. Top with lettuce. Top with the remaining bread halves, if using whole wheat bread. Makes 1 serving.

Chicken-Salsa-Topped Potato

312 calories/serving

Potatoes without butter and sour cream are a nutritious choice for the dieter.

1 medium baking potato
½ of a 5-ounce can chunk-style white meat chicken
¼ cup chili salsa
⅛ teaspoon onion powder

● Up to 6 hours before mealtime, scrub potato; prick with a fork. Place in a clear plastic bag; seal. In a custard cup stir together chicken, chili salsa, and onion powder. Securely cover with clear plastic wrap. Pack potato, chicken-salsa mixture, a microwave-safe paper plate or a nonmetal plate, a paper towel, a knife, a fork, and a spoon to take along in an insulated lunch box with an ice pack.

● At mealtime, on the microwave-safe paper plate or nonmetal plate micro-cook unwrapped potato, uncovered, on 100% power (HIGH) for 3 to 5 minutes or till nearly done, rotating once. Let the potato stand, uncovered, for 5 minutes to finish cooking.

● Meanwhile, vent the clear plastic wrap that covers the chicken-salsa mixture by leaving a small area unsealed at the edge of the custard cup. Micro-cook on 100% power (HIGH) for 1 to 2 minutes or till heated through.

● When potato is done, gently roll the potato under your hand to loosen the pulp. Cut a lengthwise slit in the top of the potato. Press the ends and push up. Spoon chicken-salsa mixture into the potato. Makes 1 serving.

Oriental Chicken Soup

144 calories/serving

Other leftover meats, such as beef or pork, also work well in this soup. If you substitute beef, use beef bouillon granules.

⅔ cup water
½ cup chopped cooked
  chicken
1 small carrot, thinly bias
  sliced (¼ cup)
2 teaspoons soy sauce
¼ teaspoon instant chicken
  bouillon granules
  Dash crushed red pepper
  Dash ground ginger

● Up to 6 hours before mealtime, in a 1-quart casserole stir together water, chicken, carrot, soy sauce, bouillon granules, red pepper, and ginger. Micro-cook, covered, on 100% power (HIGH) for 5 to 6 minutes or till boiling, stirring once. Spoon soup into a small vacuum bottle; seal. Pack soup and a spoon to take along. Makes 1 serving.

Vegetable Rarebit

259 calories/serving

Add some fresh fruit to your brown-bag lunch. It makes a delicious accompaniment to this crispy, open-face sandwich.

¼ cup coarsely shredded
  cabbage
1 small stalk celery, chopped
  (¼ cup)
2 small radishes, chopped
  (about 3 tablespoons)
½ of a small carrot, chopped
  (about 3 tablespoons)
1 tablespoon calorie-reduced
  French salad dressing
2 slices American cheese
  spread (1½ ounces total)
1 slice firm-textured whole
  wheat bread, toasted and
  halved diagonally
2 tablespoons fresh alfalfa
  sprouts

● Up to 6 hours before mealtime, toss together cabbage, celery, radishes, carrot, and salad dressing. Place in a clear plastic bag; seal tightly. In 3 separate clear plastic bags pack the cheese slices, toasted bread halves, and alfalfa sprouts; seal. Pack the cabbage mixture, cheese slices, bread, alfalfa sprouts, a micro-wave-safe paper plate or a nonmetal plate, and a fork to take along in an insulated lunch box.
● At mealtime, place bread halves on the microwave-safe paper plate or the nonmetal plate. Top with the cabbage mixture. Place the cheese slices atop the cabbage mixture, tearing to fit. Micro-cook, uncovered, on 100% power (HIGH) about 1 minute or till the cheese begins to melt. Top with the alfalfa sprouts. Makes 1 serving.

Vegetable Rarebit

Frankfurter in a Pita

347 calories/serving

The traditional frankfurter in a bun is reduced by 116 calories when you use a chicken frankfurter and pita bread.

1   chicken frankfurter, cut into
      ¼-inch slices
2   slices American cheese, torn
      into small pieces (1½
      ounces total)
½   of a small tomato, chopped
      (¼ cup)
1   tablespoon chopped onion
2   teaspoons sweet pickle
      relish
½   of an 8-inch pita bread
      round

● Up to 6 hours before mealtime, in a large custard cup combine the chicken frankfurter, cheese, tomato, onion, and sweet pickle relish; securely cover with clear plastic wrap. In a clear plastic bag place the pita bread half; seal. Pack frankfurter mixture, pita half, and a spoon to take along in an insulated lunch box with an ice pack.
● At mealtime, micro-cook frankfurter mixture, uncovered, on 100% power (HIGH) for 1½ to 2 minutes or till heated through, stirring once. Spoon the frankfurter mixture into the pita half. Makes 1 serving.

Packing a Brown Bag

● Plan ahead when packing a brown bag. Think about what essentials you will need at mealtime and pack those first. Will you need a napkin, a paper plate, plastic utensils, and/or a paper cup?
● Pack for safety. Pack sharp utensils individually. Consider a food's susceptibility to bacterial growth when packing a brown bag. Pack to keep cold foods cold and warm foods warm.

● Pack for convenience. Disposability is a big plus for the brown bagger. Although polystyrene foam should not go into the microwave oven, you may want to save the covered cups and bowls from the delicatessen for later use in packing a brown bag.
● Pack to retain the appeal of the food. To keep moist foods moist and dry foods dry, wrap foods separately in clear plastic bags or in clear plastic wrap. If you have a juicy sandwich filling, pack it separately and assemble the sandwich at mealtime.

Nutrition Analysis

	CALORIES	PROTEIN (g)	CARBOHYDRATE (g)	FAT (g)	SODIUM (mg)	POTASSIUM (mg)	PROTEIN	VITAMIN A	VITAMIN C	THIAMINE	RIBOFLAVIN	NIACIN	CALCIUM	IRON
	Per Serving						Percent U.S. RDA Per Serving							
Main Dishes, Beef														
Barbecue Beef Tortillas (p. 10)	339	38	23	7	595	347	58	17	10	10	18	32	9	32
Beef and Tomato Sandwich (p. 87)	266	22	27	9	1892	405	34	18	25	14	16	16	18	23
Beef Pastitsio (p. 51)	191	17	12	8	522	234	27	12	6	8	15	16	10	12
Beef-Vegetable Pockets (p. 58)	244	20	24	7	931	367	31	47	36	12	14	21	6	21
Beef-Vegetable Soup for Two (p. 58)	149	14	12	5	1074	284	22	77	36	10	11	21	3	13
Fiesta Burgers (p. 63)	248	23	16	10	1072	518	36	25	18	13	17	25	7	21
Italian Beef and Vegetables (p. 10)	149	19	6	5	47	413	29	8	49	7	12	21	2	15
Italian-Style Veal Patties (p. 61)	246	23	3	15	356	254	36	7	2	9	18	31	3	17
Meatballs with Wine Sauce (p. 12)	349	30	20	15	466	956	46	24	82	18	31	41	12	31
Open-Face Chili Sandwich (p. 84)	286	27	21	10	599	389	41	11	9	14	15	33	4	24
Saucy Beef and Veal Meatballs (p. 51)	220	21	9	10	386	313	33	7	10	9	15	27	3	18
Saucy Cubed Steak (p. 60)	160	22	3	6	284	304	34	1	1	5	14	22	3	15
Savory Soup (p. 84)	259	25	17	10	980	522	39	179	21	12	16	34	4	22
Spinach-Lasagna Rolls (p. 15)	253	20	28	6	798	371	31	91	32	23	22	21	15	18
Stuffed Peppers (p. 74)	263	22	29	8	739	642	34	29	364	17	20	30	3	22
Stuffed Steak Roll and Noodles (p. 72)	376	26	33	14	612	511	40	66	5	25	20	34	5	25
Veal and Spinach Roll-Ups (p. 15)	239	25	5	13	349	652	38	115	39	16	26	40	10	27
Vegetable-Beef Stew (p. 48)	234	27	11	9	465	509	42	79	35	8	16	25	5	22
Yogurt Beef Stroganoff (p. 48)	366	33	31	12	283	606	51	5	10	19	31	39	10	25
Zucchini Lasagna (p. 52)	279	26	13	13	842	514	41	25	43	12	25	24	22	16
Main Dishes, Lamb														
Lamb Chops with Lemon-Mustard Sauce (p. 63)	119	14	1	6	203	165	22	0	3	5	8	15	1	6
Orange-Ginger Lamb Ring with Peas (p. 17)	318	18	23	17	437	366	28	14	49	21	15	18	5	15
Main Dishes, Pork														
Cranberry-Apple Glazed Ham (p. 17)	157	17	8	6	43	227	26	0	12	25	10	16	1	14
Curried Pork and Tomatoes (p. 18)	225	15	26	6	628	411	23	16	40	40	12	23	3	16
Ham and Kraut (p. 64)	210	23	12	8	605	343	35	1	20	35	16	23	4	19
Sweet-and-Sour Ham (p. 64)	145	10	20	3	176	251	16	5	14	18	7	11	2	11

Nutrition Analysis

	CALORIES	PROTEIN (g)	CARBOHYDRATE (g)	FAT (g)	SODIUM (mg)	POTASSIUM (mg)	PROTEIN	VITAMIN A	VITAMIN C	THIAMINE	RIBOFLAVIN	NIACIN	CALCIUM	IRON
	Per Serving						Percent U.S. RDA Per Serving							
Main Dishes, Poultry														
Basil Chicken Saltimbocca (p. 54)	292	44	5	10	186	113	68	10	10	13	23	76	13	16
Chicken and Dumplings with Vegetables (p. 53)	274	22	26	9	444	348	34	70	6	19	17	36	15	12
Chicken-Asparagus Pitas (p. 19)	169	21	16	2	696	448	32	13	33	12	12	36	4	14
Chicken Ramekins (p. 65)	256	23	9	14	597	213	36	11	6	7	16	20	9	12
Chicken-Salsa-Topped Potato (p. 87)	312	21	36	9	1264	818	32	23	61	14	11	31	4	13
Cornish Game Hen with Pineapple Brown Rice (p. 22)	368	32	40	9	74	239	49	25	54	22	38	52	5	23
Cranberry-Raisin Chicken (p. 20)	170	20	17	3	39	108	30	2	6	6	10	37	3	10
Elegant Chicken and Grapes (p. 78)	252	38	13	4	2	123	58	9	4	8	18	72	3	13
Frankfurter in a Pita (p. 90)	347	12	15	13	551	219	19	22	26	6	13	3	32	7
Orange-Sauced Chicken (p. 18)	216	38	4	4	180	63	58	4	21	7	17	71	2	13
Oriental Chicken Soup (p. 88)	144	24	5	3	1620	478	36	80	5	4	8	42	4	11
Peachy Chicken (p. 19)	312	40	26	4	556	94	61	8	3	14	19	77	3	18
Stuffed Cabbage Rolls (p. 76)	193	17	19	6	844	425	26	32	36	9	13	16	6	12
Stuffed Chicken Breasts (p. 80)	284	39	20	5	126	206	60	25	71	12	19	74	4	14
Tarragon Chicken (p. 65)	219	37	3	4	241	20	58	3	3	6	17	71	2	12
Turkey and Carrot Patties (p. 66)	272	42	6	8	444	556	64	38	2	8	15	65	4	13
Two-Cheese Turkey Bake (p. 81)	331	26	28	12	704	335	40	15	44	20	23	24	20	12
Main Dishes, Fish														
Calorie-Trimmed Coquilles Saint Jacques (p. 54)	236	30	19	3	658	734	46	6	7	15	17	15	22	23
Clam-Stuffed Snapper (p. 23)	285	54	5	15	506	1080	83	32	9	8	12	79	7	20
Crab Puff (p. 29)	252	23	12	12	1132	223	39	31	6	10	20	7	32	8
Curried Shrimp and Rice (p. 82)	238	23	23	4	882	231	36	7	10	7	5	13	14	21
Halibut in Vegetable Sauce (p. 26)	244	31	10	8	572	935	47	38	96	10	12	54	4	11
Halibut Mandarin (p. 69)	173	17	10	7	116	486	27	13	51	8	4	34	3	5
Hot Shrimp Salad (p. 70)	205	18	33	1	306	623	28	92	70	7	7	17	11	19
Italian-Style Fish (p. 70)	185	25	3	8	187	561	38	20	10	5	8	41	4	6
Salmon Patties (p. 66)	325	29	7	19	178	565	44	11	5	8	18	43	21	11
Scallops in White Wine Sauce (p. 24)	150	27	7	2	459	622	41	4	8	9	9	11	14	20
Seafood Stew (p. 24)	158	20	13	3	802	572	30	32	53	12	12	26	10	17
Slimmer Shrimp Newburg (p. 56)	280	18	21	14	356	241	23	9	1	12	17	12	14	11

	CALORIES	PROTEIN (g)	CARBOHYDRATE (g)	FAT (g)	SODIUM (mg)	POTASSIUM (mg)	PROTEIN	VITAMIN A	VITAMIN C	THIAMINE	RIBOFLAVIN	NIACIN	CALCIUM	IRON
	Per Serving						Percent U.S. RDA Per Serving							
Main Dishes, Fish *(continued)*														
Sweet-and-Sour-Sauced Fish (p. 56)	249	18	34	4	642	517	28	37	40	11	5	31	4	11
Tropical Tuna Melt (p. 22)	249	17	30	7	323	294	28	4	14	11	9	34	11	8
Main Dishes, Eggs and Cheese														
Cheese Manicotti (p. 26)	152	12	18	3	465	123	19	12	16	5	14	6	7	6
Ham and Egg Casserole (p. 27)	258	18	2	19	230	186	28	15	1	15	20	9	16	12
Pizza Eggs (p. 29)	225	16	7	14	658	216	25	33	25	10	26	5	14	15
Vegetable Rarebit (p. 88)	259	13	19	15	648	301	20	51	23	7	13	5	34	9
Side Dishes														
Asparagus with Herb Sauce (p. 30)	38	5	5	1	73	217	8	12	30	8	9	4	9	5
Broccoli and Onions with Cheese Sauce (p. 30)	67	5	8	3	72	252	7	39	87	4	10	2	9	3
Dilled Vegetable Medley (p. 34)	38	2	7	1	169	258	3	81	40	4	6	2	6	4
Green Pea Puree (p. 32)	53	4	9	0	94	112	6	10	23	15	5	7	2	8
Harvest Cinnamon Beans (p. 37)	44	2	10	0	51	335	4	17	42	7	8	4	7	6
Lemon-Garlic Vegetables (p. 35)	33	2	4	1	45	189	3	29	108	4	4	2	3	3
Lima Beans with Pimiento (p. 35)	90	5	15	1	129	393	7	13	53	5	3	5	2	9
Minted Carrot Puree (p. 34)	32	1	7	0	106	253	2	159	10	3	3	2	3	3
Orange-Sauced Carrots (p. 31)	76	2	18	0	60	496	2	279	43	7	4	4	5	5
Parslied Rice (p. 64)	89	2	20	0	0	0	3	0	0	7	0	4	0	4
Parsnip Puree (p. 34)	53	2	12	0	78	361	2	0	17	4	5	1	5	2
Spinach with Horseradish-Cucumber Sauce (p. 31)	63	3	5	4	55	643	5	150	46	6	9	2	11	11
Tangy Green Beans (p. 37)	64	1	11	1	28	131	2	13	27	3	4	1	3	3
Desserts														
Cantaberry Boats (p. 40)	58	1	14	0	16	394	2	90	97	4	4	5	2	5
Cocoa Mint Mousse (p. 42)	113	1	8	8	77	2	2	1	0	1	2	0	2	1
Glazed Citrus Sections (p. 42)	127	1	31	0	7	270	2	10	113	7	2	2	6	6
Harvest-of-Fruit Parfaits (p. 45)	100	1	25	0	3	194	2	5	65	5	3	2	3	4
Spiced Apple Flambé (p. 40)	151	1	31	1	4	241	1	4	38	5	2	1	2	4
Strawberries and Cheese (p. 38)	129	4	17	6	88	233	6	8	107	3	10	3	7	7
Vanilla Pears (p. 38)	151	3	29	4	60	260	4	4	12	3	6	1	3	4
Snacks and Beverages														
Hot Broccoli Dip (p. 46)	23	18	18	27	1026	638	28	122	195	10	29	6	22	10
Savory Vegetable Drink (p. 46)	32	2	7	0	380	402	3	25	27	6	3	7	2	5
Spiced Citrus Warmer (p. 45)	84	1	20	0	2	251	1	5	136	7	2	3	1	2

Index